Riff on Six:

New and Selected Poems

JAMES REISS is the author of four poetry books, the most recent of which, *Ten Thousand Good Mornings*, was nominated for the 2002 Pulitzer Prize. His work has appeared in such places as *The Atlantic Monthly*, *The New Yorker*, and *The Paris Review*, plus many anthologies, textbooks, and Web sites. He has won numerous national and regional literary awards and grants. He is Professor of English and Editor of Miami University Press in Oxford, Ohio.

Riff on Six

NEW AND SELECTED POEMS

JAMES REISS

SALT

PUBLISHED BY SALT PUBLISHING
PO Box 937, Great Wilbraham, Cambridge PDO CB1 5JX United Kingdom
PO Box 202, Applecross, Western Australia 6153

© James Reiss, 2003

The right of James Reiss to be identified as the
author of this work has been asserted by him in accordance
with Section 77 of the Copyright, Designs and Patents Act 1988.

First published 2003

Printed and bound in the United Kingdom by Lightning Source

Typeset in Swift 9.5 / 13

ISBN 1 84471 031 9 paperback

SP

1 3 5 7 9 8 6 4 2

For Mary Jo

Contents

Acknowledgments

The author is grateful to editors of the following publications, where most of the poems in this book first appeared:

Agni, The American Poetry Review, American Review, Antaeus, Antioch Review, The Atlantic Monthly, Boulevard, The Bridge, Buffalo Report, CounterPunch, Esquire, Flights, The Formalist, Hotel Amerika, The Hudson Review, The Kenyon Review, Light, Meridian, Miamian, Midstream, The Nation, The Nebraska Review, New American Review, The New Republic, The New Yorker, The New York Times, Nimrod, The Ohio Review, The Paris Review, Pequod, Poetry, Poetry Northwest, Poets Against the War, The Quarterly, The Rhetoric Review, The Saturday Review, Shenandoah, Slate, Smartish Pace, Southwest Review, Verse, Virginia Quarterly Review, Western Humanities Review.

The author wishes to thank the following publishers:

The Ecco Press: *The Breathers* (1974)
The University of Pittsburgh Press: *Express* (1983)
Carnegie Mellon University Press: *The Parable of Fire* (1996)
Carnegie Mellon University Press: *Ten Thousand Good Mornings* (2001)

The author is indebted to Creative Artists Public Service (CAPS), The Dorland Mountain Arts Colony, The MacDowell Colony, Miami University's Committee on Faculty Research, The National Endowment for the Arts, The New York Foundation for the Arts, and The Ohio Arts Council for grants and residencies that helped me write these poems.

from The Breathers (1974)

The Breathers

(Jeffrey Andrew Reiss—October 5, 1969)

In Ohio, where these things happen,
we had been loving all winter.
By June you looked down and saw your belly
was soft as fresh bread.

In Florida, standing on the bathroom
scales, you were convinced—
and looked both ways for a full minute before crossing
Brickell Boulevard.

In Colorado you waited-out summer in a mountain
cabin, with Dr. Spock,
your stamps, and my poems in the faint
8000-foot air.

Listen, he had a perfect body,
right down to his testicles, which I counted.
The morning he dropped from your womb, all rosy
as an apple in season, breathing the thick
fall air of Ohio, we thought good things would happen.

Believe me, Dr. Salter and the nurses were right:
he was smell but feisty—they said he was
feisty. That afternoon in his respirator
when he urinated it was something to be proud of.
Cyanotic by evening, he looked like a dark rose.

Late that night you hear . . .

Think of the only possible twentieth-century consolations:
Doris saying it might have been better this way;
think of brain damage, car crashes, dead soldiers.
Better seventeen hours than eighteen, twenty years
of half-life in Ohio where nothing happens.

Late that night you hear them
in the . . .

For, after all, we are young, traveling
at full speed into the bull's eye of the atom.
There's a Pepsi and hot dog stand in that bull's eye,
and babies of the future dancing around us.
Listen, the air is thick with our cries!

Late that night you hear them
in the nursery, the breathers.
Their tiny lungs go in and out like the air
bladder on an oxygen tank
or the rhythm of sex.
Asleep, your arms shoot towards that target
with a stretch that lifts you like a zombie,
wakes you to the deafening breathers.

And now you see them crawling
rings around your bed, in blankets,
buntings, preemies in incubators circling
on casters, a few with cleft palates, heart trouble,
all feistily breathing, crawling
away from your rigidly outstretched arms—
breathing, robbing the air.

The Green Tree

Ever since my daughters started to walk
I have had increasing difficulty with my eyes.
I remember the day Wendy took her first steps, when
she said "bamboo" and waddled over to pat the rusty bumper

of a truck, I could barely make out the writing
scrawled in dirt on the trailer and had trouble focusing
as she stepped into its shadow.
The morning in Maine when she raced down the beach

and splashed into the ocean before I could reach her,
I actually mistook her for another little girl in pink
whom—I am sorry to say—I began leading slowly out of the
      water.
Then there is Jill: when she first walked I remember

looking at her and thinking, "I am a camera fading back, back."
Years later when she would go rollerskating with Wendy
my eyes were so bad I could no longer tell
where the sidewalks left off and my daughters began.

By now everything has faded into fine print. I
have been to a doctor who says he is also troubled,
but has sons. My only son died one day after
birth, weighing two pounds. His name was

Jeffrey, but I have always preferred to call him "Under-the-Earth"
or, especially on rainy days, "Under-the-Sod." In fact,
sometimes I catch myself repeating these words: "My only son,
Under-the-Sod, is playing over there by the green tree."

The Blue Snow

Right now, somewhere, someone is thinking of you.
Lifting her arms into the summer
evening, or folding a letter in a small room,
someone is thinking your name and quietly saying:

"You came into my life on the 23rd
after dinner, when light fell through the window so starkly
you said it reminded you of a Japanese painting
called The Blue Snow, and I laughed, thinking,

who is this man who talks like a poet?"
Now, while it is still light, someone
is stepping out of her dress and thinking:
"I will turn off every light in this house

and lie down naked in front of my mirror till dawn,
then go to the window with the early morning sun on my
         breasts—
waiting for you who will never come by, you
who have forgotten what it is to be lonely."

The Post Card

The summer Barbara gave birth I received a post
card from someone I'd never heard of, Mrs. Sidney Burns,
postmarked August 4th from someplace I'd never heard of in
      Iowa.
In a shaky third-grade script these words were penciled:

    "have bin thinkin of you how do you like all this winter
    now you think of me once in a wile mr. reece what will
    become of the ice house

                    mrs. sidney burns"

On the back a cheap imitation of a Currier
and Ives Christmas scene: by a tiny road a gingerbread
farmhouse in the snow with long
icicles hanging from the roof over the windows
and the faintest outline of a woman's face in one window,
      behind
the curtain of icicles, as though someone
had penciled it in and then decided to erase it.

People in Sunlight

A man and a woman are sitting
on an overstuffed sofa
in a room overflowing with sunlight—
she in a black bikini,

he in a soldier's uniform.
He takes off his cap and says her husband
was a good soldier.
She crosses her legs and says that may be

true as the sky is blue.
He unpins a miniature flag from his sleeve
and presents her with it.
Sunlight catches the stripes, tossing

them all over the rug like spilled coffee.
Sunlight catches the coffee
table off-guard, tossing
it back in their faces.

She touches her lips to the flag
and says she's hungry.
He fiddles with his buttons
and says nothing.

She unbuttons her bikini and stands
in a block of sunlight, grinning.
He grins, too; it is a beautiful day,
the War is almost over.

Come Out, Come Out!

(Joseph Reiss: 1908–1970)

1

Looking at those snapshots of last August, I see
the emphysema in your eyes, the barrel chest, hump
back, and pot belly of its final stages.
As you bend by the bird feeder, pressing your fist
into your stomach to squeeze air out of those New York City
     lungs,
or pose by the pool of your April-new Florida house
with your poodle, Pepe—you look like a miracle of wonder
drugs and Bennett machines.

By September you began talking about an article for *Life*
called "I Have Emphysema"
but never made it past the words scribbled in your journal
the morning after an attack so bad
it took you an hour to crawl to your machine
halfway across the bedroom: "Wheezing is my constant
     companion.
I ask for life. I beg for it. O Lord in thy dwelling place,
it slips through my hands like a fish."

2

Are you out there, Dad? Like in the old days when you came
    home from work with penny boxes of Chiclets?

Well, if you're out there like on another DC-3 business trip to
    Chicago, don't worry, I'll find you, Dad.

3

When my father died his face turned blue,
blue as the sky, I thought, and went
outside to find him in a bird.
Enormous swarms of purple birds
were headed home. The sky grew dark—
dark as his wrists, I thought, his wrists!

4

Looking at those snapshots of last August, I see
the vacant after-dinner gaze
of a man who is drowning in mid-air:
behind him the expensive bird feeder
that attracted only starlings—Mafia birds,
he called them—scaring the songbirds away;
alongside him the pool he never used,
the barbecue from Sears, and Pepe . . .

By September you began reading poetry again,
borrowing my Strand anthology
and loving it so much
that afterwards no one could find it.
Painter of women with heart-shaped faces, you knew the poetry
of drugs with exotic names like Celestone and Serax;
in September you wrote: "O secret journal, there is no one
to tell this to: the nights are worst in the cage."

5

When my father died the day turned red
with sirens and doctors pronouncing him dead.
The wind broke down and the sun stood still.
In Florida I found a hill
and looked out over the Everglades
where the moon was as white as aspirin.

6

Are you out there, Dad? Like one of your Mafia birds swirling
over that spot off Lighthouse Cove where we dropped your
ashes from a boat—

Out there sailing in a summer's breeze, skipping over the ocean
like in the Midnight Cowboy song we sang on the stern as
you slipped through our fingers?

7

The sun went down and the moon blew up.
Then I found my father on the floor
of an ocean of stars like a fish
whose veins were grayer than ash,
whose half-open eyes were covered with silt,
whose split tongue sang like a stone.

8

You disappeared into your paintings, papers, and the genes of
your grandchildren. My Yahrzeit candle smothers in wax.

It is dark in the closet where you have spanked me and left me,
but I can still feel the slap of your hand like a kiss on the
mouth.

Even Now

My mother always had such blond
hair that my father used to say he could see it through a
    telephone.
Calling from Union
Station, he would swear he could see it all the way from
    Chicago.
I have tried to imagine her in our old

    apartment, putting down the receiver and looking
        westward through smog
    across the Hudson River into a ball of sun less gold
    than her hair.
    For years I have tried to remember the way my father
    dropped his r's and said *very frankly*

or *heddo*, instead of hello, when he answered the phone.
Yet even while they were alive and I brought them flowers,
when he would wag his red
face in my face and talk about the Second World
War—even then I always made sure I carried

    their wallet-sized photos.
    Even as I write this there is a photo on my desk
    of them mugging like kids
    next to some playground swings in the snow.
    My father seems about to hurl a gigantic snowball,

and my mother's mouth is shaped like an O.
No! she is protesting, her hair hidden in a fur cap.
But see, it is already snowing so hard
the flakes are falling like asterisks.

On Hot Days

Remember those X-ray machines in shoe stores
where you put your feet under green light
and gazed at your foot bones like huge
    goldfish in an acquarium

and it was quiet and your mother looked on
with her Roosevelt button while the sweat-smelling
salesman with the Yiddish accent and the splotched
    face hovered like a giant

amoeba above you and grinned, *Okay, sonny*
and your mother nudged you, because X-rays
could be dangerous, so you sat in the big
    chair by the window that faced

the El while the salesman lugged box after box
of fresh-smelling shoes from the back room,
lacing them to you like cool bags of water,
    and you squished to the mirror—

Captain Frogman with your swim
fins and rubber suit to protect you
from the icy terror of the deep green
    sea—so that when the salesman

grinned and turned off your X-ray vision you asked
for yet another cooler pair to swim in
and when he finally shook his shoehorn
    at you and frowned, his face

one fiery splotch of cordovan, your mother
winced and pulled you into the heat
of the street just as the El burst overhead
    like a thunderclap.

¿Habla Usted Español?

The Spanish expression *Cuando yo era muchacho*
may be translated: when I was a boy,
as, for example, "When I was a boy I wanted to be
a train driver," or "When I was a boy I was completely unaware
      of the flimsy orchid of life."
It is the kind of expression found in textbooks of the blue breeze
and is more useful, really, than expressions like "Please put the
      bananas on the table, Maria,"
or "Take it easy is the motto of the happy-go-lucky Mexican."
When I was a boy the sun was a horse.
When I was a boy I sang "Rum and Coca-Cola."
When I was a boy my father told me the mountains were the
      earth's sombreros.

This Poem

I died, and my mother put this poem in a desk drawer.
She opened the drawer slowly.
She placed the poem inside like a cut flower.
Inside, among pencils and an old photograph, this poem lay
    hidden for years.

One day a man came looking for matches.
By now my mother had died, too, and the man had come to
    move the desk.
He opened the drawer and found this poem.
He lifted it out like a cracked china bowl.
He read it, pointing to the yellowed words, saying them under
    his breath.
He did not understand it.
But he took it home to you, his father, who folded it in a book.

Today this poem is not a poem but a wheat field.
An old man, you are sitting by a window when you realize this.
A wind seems to blow through the wheat of these words.
This poem is unfolding, flowering in your hands.

Crystal

A man wets his forefinger with his tongue and holds
up a perfect water glass, empty and glistening.
He is sitting at a table in a large
hall with other men in identical blue

blazers with eagle medallions over their breast pockets.
Now the first man fingers the glass
rim, tentatively, as if it were jagged-edged.
And now he strokes it clockwise, slowly, stopping

to wet his finger again and again, like an old
man paging through a book—until the glass
comes to life with a thin, high whine like nothing
he has ever heard, and the others look up in amazement,
        catching

on, holding up their glasses, too, wetting and stroking
them clockwise like ice skaters in unison.
All the glasses are coming to life now; their throats are
slowly catching fire, glistening with a thinner,

higher whine than any bird. It is like a pitch
pipe with wings. It is something like the music each
man heard when he stepped outside at night
for the first time alone as a boy. Then

there was nothing in the sky but stars and music.
And the sky was like glass.

from Express (1983)

A Candy Store in Washington Heights

One of those two-bit luncheonettes on a nothing
block with Coca-Cola
signs and an owner who looks like Groucho Marx.
One of those holes in the heat
wall of summer
up the hill from the bridge and its lighthouse.
One of those prewar leftovers
that specialize in Hamilton Beach malted mixers
and fans on the ceiling
where BLTs were always
a quarter and the owner, Levine, still stoops
with a cigar that has been rotting
in his hand for thirty years.

> *Levine of the gray suspenders,*
> *Levine of the white shirt in summer that is always fading,*
> *Levine of the brown teeth and baldspot, scooping ice cream*
>   *from your old horse of a freezer:*

By the magazine rack,
by the blackening collection of comics
and dustmice, a boy who has paid for his malted
with his palms up, letting
you dip for dimes,
has his nose in *Wonder Woman*.
Today he will sneak it under his T-shirt.
While you are screwing the ketchup
or cursing the Germans,
he will slink out the door
                    with the turn
of your cheek.

Locked in his bedroom
for hours, he will pore over "Wonder
Woman in Jersey City," "Batman
Trapped in the Cave of Lost Guano"—
and will rise to his mother's
shouts for dinner only when the scraps
of paper on his desk tell everything
he knows about bridges in sunlight.

> *Levine of the frankfurter fingers,*
> *Levine of the dishrag and dills,*
> *Levine of the Life Savers, Charms, the small cherry Cokes*
> *that are never enough:*

In one of those dustbins
swept up from the gutters of streets
not far from the river that summer,
I stole the cigar from your mouth
and the hundred wads of Chiclets
stuck under your counter.

I stuffed them under my T-shirt.
I kneaded them in my pocket.
I shaped them into a bridge.
I sat at my desk as I shaped
the sun-silver towers, the roadway,
the lighthouse red as a matchtip—
for you, Levine, for you.

Approaching Washington Heights

North, near the tip, where the island
raises its head like a factory
worker who has been asleep in a gray cap
and who blinks, his eyes full of sand
his lips chapped with age

where the only bridge in America
that can sing "Ol' Man River" with the wind
in its cables has an audience of fire
escapes, and the brown ledge
of the land sprouts names
like Chittenden Avenue, Cabrini Boulevard

I who have driven three decades of A trains
shotgun to the motorman from midtown
glued to the window
as we highballed sixty blocks without a stop
up the guts of an electric eel

north past stray stations, dimwatted,
mudugly, platforms
that would be the rust-colored scenarios
of nightmares in which I would race
to catch a train but never make it
my legs churning in the same spot

I who am churning now, who have stayed
on, not gotten off pale-faced
in Harlem as if in the middle of a sentence

I who will never get off this train
of thought, these silver wheels
                              barreling
north toward the black mammoth elevators
and hammering escalators of 181st Street

where the man who sells tokens has a life
behind bars totally alien
from mine, though his face is also a map
of Israel, his eyes are tiny
dead seas

Sueños

In my dreams I always speak Spanish.
The cemetery may be in Brooklyn,
and I may be kneeling on a rise
looking out at the skyline of the city,
but I will whisper, *Mira el sol.*

And it is true the late morning
sun will turn that bank of skyscrapers
the color of bleached bone in Sonora,
and all the window washers of Manhattan
will white-out like a TV screen

in Venezuela turning to snow.
But the gray face on the headstone photograph
has a nose like my father's,
and his voice had the lilt of the ghettos
of central Europe.

So I should kneel lower and say something
in Yiddish about fathers, grandfathers,
the hacked limbs of a family tree
that reaches as high as Manhattan.
I should say, *Grampa, I loved those times*

we ran through the underpasses in Central
Park, you with your cane, I with my ice
cream cones, shouting for echoes,
bursting out into sunlight—
if I only knew the language to say it in.

Brothers

Eighteen years you beat me over the head
with the butt end of our brotherhood.
So where are you now, Mr. Top
Dog on the Bunk Bed, Mr. Big
Back on the High School Football Team?

You hauled ass out of that town
with its flimsy goalposts.
Now you're down there with your Dead
Sea, your Jerusalem, busy
with the same old border disputes

that sparked our earliest fist fights.
Israel is just another locked toy
closet on your side of the bedroom, split
by electric train tracks. It's as if
you never left home at all: Yesterday

in a bar in Washington Heights
I saw a man who could have been you.
The Jets were playing the Steelers with two
downs to go, and in the icy
lightshow of smoke

he lifted a pitcher of beer
and swilled it just as the screen
blazed red with an ad for Gillette.
And I thought, Here is my blood brother
whose only gifts to me were kicks

in the teeth, his cast-off comic books,
and worst of all, wrapped, sharpened
for a lifetime,
the perfect razor of my rage.

A Day in Ohio

The painters began work on the house,
wielding their brushes like wings.
By noon they took off their caps
and blotted their brows with tan rags,
then lit cigarettes by striking wooden
matches on their boots in long slow arcs.

The roof took on the color of the sun
as it broke yolk-like on the weather vane.
They did not see it splatter.
Bronze in their five-o'clock shadows,
they slapped one last gold stroke
and lowered their scaffold and stretched.

By the Steps of the Metropolitan Museum of Art
(For Thomas Lux)

Choking with silent laughter, the chalk-faced mime
jousts with the crowd, grabs a smiling sailor,
and sets him on his knees before a school-
girl posed with a rose in her teeth.
The crowd explodes, and the air
is charged with the jingle of loose change.

A driver waiting for the light to change
pulls to the curb and tosses the mime
a silver coin that glitters in midair
before dropping at the feet of the sailor,
making him smile more widely and show his teeth
like a politician visiting a high school.

I drift and think of a dancing school
I drove my daughters to. I watched them change
into shy swans, gifted to the teeth
with graceful napes and wrists—just as the mime
is graceful in his placement of the sailor
whose smile unwinds in the afternoon air

when all at once an air-
raid siren I haven't heard since public school
starts shrieking from some roof. The sailor
takes off with the pigeons, unsmiling for a change.
The schoolgirl puts fingers in her ears. The mime
pretends he's screaming, gritting his teeth.

It is like fingernails down chalkboards setting teeth
on edge, this siren slicing the air.
People scatter. Even the mime
slinks uptown, and the school-
girl disappears without her rose—as if she could change
my image of her with the sailor

at her feet, that skittery peacoated sailor,
both blushing red as the rose in her teeth,
posed statuelike without change . . .
I leave the museum to escape the air-
raid siren. Up the street school
buses idle, double-parked, and I notice the mime,

the chalk-faced mime, outside my daughters' school
in the three-o'clock air. He lists like a sailor,
whistles through his teeth, and begs for change.

New York Is My City

Here where the wind from New Jersey
dumps buckets of ice on the skin
of the river and rooftop clotheslines bell
like flags in a schoolyard
of shouters punchball players and girls
skipping rope to a silent count

where every cobblestone that brightens
in the sun confirms my grandparents' belief
these streets are paved with gold
and chalk marks on the sidewalk spell
hopscotch in any language

I am king of the hill
hoisted shoulder-high over 181st Street
by every aproned butcher and candystore man
every loose-footed elevator operator
out of work in a neighborhood
of six-story walkups

Here where merely to walk down
to the river is an experience
etched in azure never gray
the Palisades shoot up in their leather jacket
of sunlight and frame a painting

of a boy hefted by sweat-spangled elders
who arrived in this city on ships
in rag shirts and European shoes
and made the sidewalks leap to meet their feet
that now tramp riverward
past their fishstores and fruitstands

Here where the tarred and feathery land
dips to a ballfield a tarmac
under the struts of a steel suspension bridge
I am lifted seaward flying
over the heads of the elders who have borne

the burden of my youth smiling and only now
when I am halfway to the heights
of moon mountains toss up their caps
in a geyser that reaches
Lake Tear of the Clouds

Arigato Means Thank You

This morning I woke with the word
arigato on my lips.
                    Was it Japanese?
I lay by you in a sauna
bath of sun and wondered why *arigato*
instead of *breasts* or *silence*.
I had never loved language
more than the night I learned your breasts
were vessels of silence.
                    Still,
I would never dream of saying things
like *Will you have saki, darling?*
I had certainly never taken a course
in foreign correspondences or the exotic
marriage of orange and gold possible
through sunny curtains.
                    Yet here I lay
on a brightening plain, saying
arigato over and over
                    until you
slid out of your pale kimono
of sleep and spoke to me in many tongues.

Elegy for Jay Silverheels (1920–1980)

The night the Lone Ranger got shot and you leaped onto the
screen
lithe as a wildcat in black-and-white TV buckskin with
tomahawk
I had just that day learned the word *tonto* in Spanish means
stupid.
Class had let out, and I thought,
So this is what they call you for helping a good guy,
tripping up crooks in a grownup schoolyard.
Now I am grownup and finger the silver
bullet of my accomplishments as a poor excuse for another
person's hand.
I gallop to do good, I jog to capture a sunrise,
and as sure as whitewall tires line a side street I am a masked
man.

If only I could throw off this sadness, my heavy headdress,
and build a fire and smoke a pipe for our ancestors
who rode this planet's saddle side by side:
Sidekicks with winged heels,
they were stupid, they shot for the sun.

Pumas

A woman in a mauve dress mentions
her passion for pumas
I nod gravely and say
I saw a puma cross

outside my window once
years ago holed-up at a writers' colony
Out of the woods it stalked through the snow
pausing to lift each paw

Then topics shift
We move toward the bar and branch off
in separate directions

Later I wonder what she meant
If I who never saw a puma
or anything that winter but my bloated self
crouching in an outhouse mirror
was capable of such snowy untruth
what veils her words must also wear

Express

In the indigo nightlight of a Pullman roomette
I climb down from my tangle-blanketed berth
to sun in the glow from the bulb.
I bathe in a bucket of color. Ultraviolet
in the washroom mirror, I whisper
I am Little Boy Blue—
until, inches away in your lower berth,
you mumble through your mustache, Back to bed.

I check the porter's door for shined shoes,
then climb out of my slippers,
thinking, The sheep's in the meadow—
while the wheels' iambic clack
and the steam engine's whistle
doppler in the ears of drivers
caught at crossings as bells clang red
outside the plate-glass window where you lie.

I dream you stare at vineyards spinning past
until you merge with the Mohawk River Valley,
enveloping grape-grown hills
with one expansive sweep of your arm.
Wine-blue over woolly shadows
of silos in the rain,
you balance track and train on your pajama sleeve
and rock them like a baby.

Swaddled in fog, I am your second son
counting cows in the corn, the river's willows,
while lamps from farmers' parlors glint.
It is four A.M. when you hold me
closer to your vintage breath to mouthe
a lullaby: fish and lumber, coal and hay,
two hundred miles on the Erie Canal—
until morning finds us in a polychrome city.

FATHER

Yes, morning found us mostly sunny and mild.
When you grabbed my hand in a taxi
and said, "Look at the Eastman Kodak buildings, Dad,"
I felt as though I'd never seen a skyline: The mist
from Genessee Falls rainbowed,
and the glint off Kodak's red-brick compound
hit me so hard I felt giddy
and overtipped our driver.

I'd known mornings at home by the window
when the river winked through coal
smoke from the Hudson Line
so invitingly I'd wanted to drop my portfolio
and cancel my appointments.
In chiaroscuro New York
I'd photographed "Empire Shade" and "Umber Cathedral."
How could I know Rochester would be rain-washed and
        resplendent?

We leaned on a breeze and made haste
to a conference room where a buyer
sat for our sales show of travel scenes.
But while you fidgeted beside me at the table
that faced a photomural of palm trees and sand dunes,
I thought, For all the lushness of our love
—how I bloomed for you, my second son—
I was a spiny cactus for your brother.

Him I adored until his mother's kiss
found me jealous, hateful.
Hospitalized with asthma the day he graduated kindergarten,
I lay in an oxygen tent,
dreaming my Brownie stills burned in their albums.
Your brother's baby pictures curled aflame.
His bonnet bulged, his crib and diapers crisped
in the incandescent air.

OLDER SON

Yet I survived without skin grafts
or curses for your bad moods, Father. Spite
was your woodshed—no whipping post but a week
of silence at the desk or dinner table.
You greeted me with frosty glares that made
your mustache and chinless jaw
look like a painting of Satan
in a book I'd begun.

[37]

I read a hundred books, but none expressed
my feelings, none aroused my ire so much
as two words, "darkness visible": The room in the basement
where you developed negatives in hypo,
panning under a red bulb,
was an inferno of stillborn faces
munching Uneeda Biscuits
or brushing with Ipana Toothpaste.

Hung up to dry, your shots of smiles,
your tinted vistas of clouds for American Airlines,
mocked any love you might have wished to express.
Yet you emerged in the clear yellow light
of the kitchen and put your arm around my brother's shoulder.
You took him on business trips while I hung back
or played jazz that lifted me high off the piano stool
to a Jerusalem of pure feeling.

Now I quicken in a duplex with a view
of the Arab Quarter: My window overlooks
a stretch of desert tenanted by Moslems.
I shop in bazaars where veiled women scorn cameras,
selling hummus and falafel to my wife and children.
I stare west between the Suez Canal
and Italy's boot—seven thousand miles—until
I conjure your face, sky-blue in rigor mortis,
and kiss the frozen shutters of your eyelids.

Nixon

1

The sweat beaded through his makeup,
and we saw he was nervous about something we would never
      fathom.
When he turned to face Kennedy, the camera caught
a five-o'clock shadow that belied everything he said,
jawboning about toughness, nuclear muscle.
The clock on the studio wall might have ticked backward.
The spotlight might have trained on an earlier rebuttal.
Presto: He is poised over a podium
in his high-school gym, debating the ethics of sex
with a sophomore whose librarian's hairdo
suggests her point of view.
"We should consider sex not only as procreation," he says,
"but as something worth dying for."
He steps down to polite applause, but even the gym
teacher snickers and elbows the assistant coach:
"Ha! That guy's gotta be kidding. What's
his name again?"

2

The standard joke about his middle name
was that it was Miltown. Those were tranquil days
when everyone had a checkered career. Khruschev growled
      about peaceful
coexistence one minute, then took off his shoe
and slammed it down on a baize-covered desk,
while we listened on car radios
or paused over pretzels and watched on TV,
less struck by the crazy Russian bear
than by the straight man in the Brooks Brothers suit.
He was there like a brand name, entitled to such exposure
because of his special endowment, his stiff upper lip.

3

Somewhere between Whittier and Washington
he began to develop bad posture and look like Howdy
Doody, though he had no freckles
and his chin did not pop up and down on a string.
He was nobody's puppet. The little shaver
had been a Navy man who tasted sea
spray till it chapped his lips and blew holes in his theories.
Indeed, it was the sea that brought him out
of his shell: During sentry duty on deck
one night he felt something drop from his uniform
and bent with a flashlight.
It might have been the dizzies from the salt air
that hit him—he wasn't sure.
The only thing he knew was that it looked
like a husk or shell. But when he turned it over
all he could remember before fainting was touching
a masklike rubber duplicate of his face.

4

Let us assume two parties are vying to buy the Dodge mansion
on Fifth Avenue: Would you side
with those who would keep the property intact
as an aviary and a landmark? Or would you favor
those who would raze it to throw up a highrise?
Such questions he encountered daily
in water-cooler nooks and offices
that bubbled with gossip about Alger Hiss.
Yet he never forgot that night on the deck and felt infused
with new power. This added to his charm, his growing
dissatisfaction with the limits of the legal
profession. He listened to classical music and thought
how fine it would be to win a land war in Asia.

5

If "let me make one thing perfectly clear" was his motto,
could we assume his aim was clarity, if not candor?
Such questions nagged him, too. One day at the White House
he realized what he'd been saying for the past ten minutes
was bullshit—and he said so with gusto.
An aide shook his hand and left.
For once the Oval Office was empty.
He wanted to put both feet up on his desk
and say, "Ladies and gentlemen, thanks a lot."
Instead, he strolled past the window, hands clasped behind him,
and made the call to invade Cambodia.

6

He put down the phone and stared out the window. Julie's
          wedding
in the Rose Garden would be matched by the funeral of
          Watergate,
the ghost years at San Clemente and Key Biscayne
where the ocean forgave no one.
He would outlive Khruschev and Mao.
He would come into his own. He would rise
above his memoirs as swiftly as he had said goodbye to his
          mentor.
Ike had developed bedsores and called for a nurse,
but he had to get back to the White House, so he said,
"Hey, Ike, did you hear the one about the drunk caddy?"
And when Ike didn't seem to hear,
he said, "So long, fella."

Anna's Song

By now the Master was deaf and went on working
when I called him to dinner.
He would sit at the piano
and time a sonata
to a game of hide-and-seek
he played with his shadow cast
in candlelight on the carpet.

I would be sweeping or cleaning the keys
in ascending stepladders of sound
when he would crash in scattering
bits of music paper like confetti scribbling
me lovenotes deathnotes notes
about how the music of Handel made him think of linden

rows outside a noisy beerhall
until I swear I could taste beer in those trees
could smell the foam of ale in glasses
raised to the whitewooded branches.
Then he would play something and make me sit
on his tattered sparrow of a couch and call me queen
of the Rhine ignoring my steelgray hair

my face an apron of wrinkles.
And I would listen and it would be the coronation
waltz of the pinetree prince in the mill town
where I was a girl and braided my hair.
Piggytails my lover called me long ago pulling
me down on the pineneedles.

I remember peeking out from under the boughs
later trying to look tough
pretending I knew how to smoke
as the sun came up over the waxworks glazing
the chimney pots.
Even then I wanted to cry hosanna
to the pigeons and sing immortal songs.

Even then I knew the sound of legs rubbing
is a miracle of wild hush.
It is the crickets' lullaby to the moonless
shore of a pinetree island
where my lover comes to me
with pipe and timbrel.

On Learning the People's Republic of China Has Lifted Its Ban on Beethoven

A million shuttered windows in Shanghai
are opening at this moment onto wall
posters and housing projects.

Uniformed teachers and tradesmen are up
before work tuning radios
in brightening parlors.

Soon the Eroica Symphony lifts off.
Like a giant blue-green insect
iridescent over Nanking Road

it wakes nine million comrades
with the citywide thunder
rumblings of an E flat

it makes by fanning
four net-veined
pagoda-heavy wings.

~

Somewhere between blue and green
at Ellsworth Farm by the dock
where I learned to swim one summer

dragonflies disturbing the shush
of waves against the rushes made me think
of a prop plane's drumroll high

over a rice paddy where men ankle-deep
in ox piss and women balancing baskets
on their heads blended with Adirondack

cattails and marsh grass.
An oarlock popped; I could hear
my sister call our dog across the water,

but nothing mattered
except the pulse and drumroll of E flat
from the Emperor Concerto.

~

That day on Mott Street with the windows
rolled down to catch a whiff of Peking
duck and bluefish green at the gills

when you shut your eyes and leaned back
against the headrest so that your hair,
pulled tight and straight, looked Oriental

I thought of Ezra Pound at the wheel
of his wicker chair: rattan, I thought, rat-a-tat,
the buzz and clatter of horns

like "Chopsticks" banged on a baby
grand by a boy in a second-floor window.
I thought: "Chinatown streets are so narrow

I can put my feet across
and touch both curbs like a Venetian
Bridge of Sighs."

~

The wish to write about China
so that nothing distracts the reader
from the fundamental lily

is like the push to procreate
and bring up daughters to believe
a billion people sipping jasmine tea

have sweetened culture from its cradle
with spoonfuls of that black
gunpowder, meditation.

This is the sound of blackness,
the quadrophonic silence of space
when midnight throws cinder

block shadows all over
the Great Wall of China
and will not play moonlight sonatas.

~

Now the fan's eye glues me to its dream
of ice cubes, and I think
of rice paper hand fans unfolding

in formal gardens between evergreen hills
that could be called mountains.
They could be called maestros

of the north wind that beguiles us
and leaves us tranquil in valleys.
Or they could be called catafalques

of Yangtze warlords under sky-
blue pavilions. So what
are we doing in the middle

of summer, listening
to river-sweet
mandarin ramblings?

～

Again nothing matters—nothing buzzes
or clatters—only the humdrum reveille
of days when I feel my chest

cave in pressed down by a paper
tiger, a mood, not a man.
I think of a cadaverous

coolie stretched
on a bamboo pallet:
among water pipes, sallow as wax,

he puffs all day and hears the freight
train of his future go up in smoke,
concentrating on the belly

button of a manchild marbled
with bronze fat
on a prerevolutionary altar.

～

Junks and sampans are scattering
as Hong Kong harbor darkens
under whitecaps from the South China Sea

and the mainland braces for floods.
Again the bony mountains
surrounding the city are beheaded

by gray clouds,
and the Pastoral Symphony rises
from its nest

of typhoon furies. Listen,
a hundred-headed dragon is slaying a fleet
of trawlers with the whip-

lash of its forked
thunder-echoing
tongues.

Passage

1

Near South Fallsburg the woods thin out.
Broadleaf and evergreen stretches
give way to golf courses and centers for yoga.
Split-levels and rundown farms fit into a puzzle
of secondary growth—stringy Catskill birch,
ailanthus lean and hungry. One thinks of an old
swami rising from lotus position with a wand of peacock
feathers and the promise that out of this muck
of mind, this dumping ground for beer cans and despair,
one might recycle nectar.

2

My bliss leaps up like a honey-colored Bengal tiger.
Under a palmyra palm, polishing my stripes
with a sandpaper tongue,
I have dozed for decades in the shade.
I have swallowed the cobra of depression
as well as the mongoose of euphoria.
There is no end to the brush-clad plateau.
There is only the water hole where gazelles gather,
where I have sprung anew
with a saber-toothed mantra.

3

Om. A line of disciples broadens
down a carpeted aisle toward a stage.
Shoeless, from all walks, they carry baskets
of fruit, flowers, or else nickel bags of dope,
whiskey bottles—and their passage over the rug
is marked by the absence of shuffling.
Somewhere elephants with diminutive ears
munch the tender shoots of treetops
and in good time honor night's guru, Death,
by laying down their tusks and trunks quietly.

4

Out of the quiet, the windowless
dark, where I have meditated on a mat,
I will come forth chanting.
I will celebrate the fireman killed in Calcutta.
I will put no other gods before his skull
laid low by a brick. I will capture the stink
of a burnt-out storefront blackly. I will catch
the first impressions of his widow
and daughter in saris, pausing over rice,
listening to news on the wireless.

5

I will praise the peasant mother
who hitchhiked a thousand kilometers to Delhi
with four children, one an infant on her back,
only to have the authorities tell her
she must return to Ganeshpuri
to fill out more forms
before she could collect one rupee.
I will paint her thin defiant lips.
I will highlight her fine black hair and set
a crimson dot as a seal upon her forehead.

6

I will tell you the truth, friends:
Despair is no impostor. He cares not
for our rupees or rank
among beggars. He wears
all turbans and has dined with Krishna.
The bureaucracy of sin, the blind
corridors of religion, are familiar to him.
I tell you, friends,
he leaves work at close of day
like many another slaughtered cow.

7

He bikes past a couple of Brahman
bulls unyoked on the road: Hondas
honk, men in Nehru caps
lean out of car windows and jeer in Hindi
while the bulls graze nonplussed, their humps abob.
He pedals past the Portuguese consulate and a lawn
party of British naval officers raising a toast
in honor of Bombay gin. They lift glasses
to the sun as it drops over the Arabian Sea—
ever westward toward London.

8

Just so, Despair has vanished into the brush
outside of South Fallsburg. By a bridge
over a spillway, I sat cross-legged on a bench
and shut my eyes. I saw
him coast on his English racer, ashen with fatigue,
into a scrubby grove of birch and ailanthus.
I recall geese honking and the fact
that the lake's name, Nityananda,
kept echoing on my tongue
like curry and coriander.

9

I recall glancing up
at an orange-robed swami leading a band
of disciples through a glass-enclosed
walkway toward an auditorium.
The passage was narrow, cramped,
yet they glided by with room to spare—
two of them preceded the swami,
walking backwards, chatting with him,
and hefting sitars.
A conch shell blew, and we were summoned in.

10

In. Far-reaching Conch Shell whose note
calls forth chariot lines of warriors in the *Gita*
as well as a darshan line, you have summoned me in
from landscapes of distress
to meditate on higher consciousness.
You have lured me away from animal flesh
and the smell of guilt,
which have plagued my people since Noah's monsoon.
Now I put my lips to your mouth and blow
a long low note.

11

I, too, am a husk reincarnate.
I, too, am an echo of waves crashing: the Bay
of Bengal sings in my veins.
Dinghies bobbing among supertankers
compose a refrain my pulse and economics know.
I, too, am sounding a call
among boat people of all castes.
Let us launch a pleasure craft
whose only mode of power, sails notwithstanding,
is the intensity of our bliss.

12

Ah, Conch Shell, your single note, Om,
recalls a day in Mexico when I went walking
on a beach and bought a conch shell from a street vender
and brought it back to my hotel balcony and blew, thinking:
Here I am at the Pacific above brown-skinned swimmers.
Then I felt a sudden tremor, a shock
of incense and rosewater,
and saw, laid out before me like a postcard,
ten thousand pilgrims bathing in the Ganges.

from The Parable of Fire (1996)

Dark Conceit

In the Parable of Fire a driver who has been dozing
lowers his car window and pitches his cigarette
into a gully at midnight. As the spark smolders
and glows under dry chaparral, the first level
of meaning may be glimpsed: literal, dim.

When a breeze fans the glimmer into a glaring
expanse, the smoke plume rises like an emblem
and sets down a bed of ash, new layers
of thought where locoweed and desert phlox
once covered the hill by the highway.

The immigrant pickers asleep in tents near the ridge
think the smoke in their dreams comes from votive
candles back home. In a ritual they curl
more tightly into burlap bags and think
their wives lie beside them

while the flames advance higher, borne
by Santa Ana winds, as if by a will.
Yet the fire storm, with every intention
of blackening trees and singeing the moon,
maps out a myth whose meaning is written on water.

Castrati in Caesar's Court

REMUS

Of all court singers Caesar loves me best.
He makes me sing to him in his atrium
after festivals and Senate meetings.
Away from his bodyguards,
he reclines on cushions.
I set a stool beside him and begin:
"Hail, Caesar, godlike, indestructible."
The higher my voice soars
the more his features soften.
"Give me your paw, Remus," he murmurs,
guiding my hand to his head
where I finger his thinning curls
and stroke his forehead smooth.

GRACCHUS

He treats me like a jester.
Fat Bacchus he calls me.
I once was a sullen boy soprano, thin
as an olive pit, well-known in Etruria.
The day his envoy entered the temple
and summoned me to him,
I knew years of learning to treat
my voice like a vestal virgin
would cost me my manhood.
Now I hide behind smiles
and fast no longer as I did back home.
At dawn I enter Caesar's wine cellar
with a key he gave me
and drink my fill, with honeyed bread.

CAIUS

Whenever he boasts about the wars
or makes me chant hymns
to Caesarion his son,
I feel his sword between my legs.
I am young; I will never again see home.
Yet I have sung with the best musicians
in the Republic, while my mother and sister
live on sesterces I send them.
In Umbria, where spring comes late
to the mountain passes, I picture them
hard by a fire whose wood I provide,
my mother carding wool,
my sister spinning.

SEPTIMUS

I am old, yet my skin is still soft,
clear as it was when his legions
stripped my countrymen of their rags
and bundled me off in a cart
as a prize capon from the provinces.
In Gaul I sang for shepherds
and begged better fare as a minstrel
than I do at his banquets in Rome.
How many cities sacked and villagers taxed
to pay for his evening repast.
Caesar never patted my knee
or called me his Gallic cantor.
The gods will set him straight
when I sing at his funeral.

Whitman at a Grain Depot

By a loading bay that smells of millet
I tell him about photos of the Okies
in pickups piled mattress-and-bedstead-high
over empty stretches reflected
in the hollows of their cheeks.

He reminds me that Mathew Brady traced
the worry lines of an earlier generation
bivouacked beside muskets, knowing no campfire
could warm fallen comrades,
no plow unplant the human harvest.

I tell him the First World War
was fought overseas by farm boys gassed
in fields seeded with mines, the orchards
ripe with snipers twenty years later.

Then was it wrong to call those barnyards lonely
because their owners were missing in action
and the horses stumbled up to their fetlocks in mud?
Is it wrong to compare corn tassels to the sun-
beaten hair of women on welfare?

A giant combine is parked by a silo here
where a spark could rain ash on our heads.
Surveying the stockpile of grain,
Whitman seizes a fistful
and calls it bone meal.

Carnegie Hill

In the cigar store where I buy lottery tickets
the man who puts my card through the computer
smiles the way I would if I'd just won millions
and decided to quit my job as a penny pincher.
A tideland squatter from Bangladesh, over the years
he's told me he lost his family to floods
in the Ganges Delta and came to this country
with a wicker suitcase and copy of the Koran.

I haven't told him about my children in college,
my wife in publishing, my dogs Hardy and Trollope
who lead me on their leashes through Central Park.
I know the wealth of the Indies resides
in brick and limestone buildings just one block
from where I live, but it could be a thousand miles.

As if he's read my thoughts, he snaps his fingers
and pulls a Monte Cruz from its humidor,
sliding it out of its cellophane wrapper,
placing its dark brown ring on his pinkie.
"Here," he says, "it's yours for a dollar even.
Forget the lottery. Have a smoke."

Memorial Quilt, Central Park

Forget that it was windy and the parched ball diamonds were
    dustbowls,
that each panel on the quilt had a name, sometimes a photo
with an inscription—"Gone but not lost"; *"Mi vida, mi alma"*—
or a pair of ballet slippers, bars from a song
composed by a man whose dates were 1950–1988
among hundreds of men, with a few women's names scattered.

James Madeiros, known as "Flash," were you speedy enough?
Peter Brierly, M.D., what good did it do you to be a physician?
Paulette without a surname, you wove
a tapestry of impressions for the mourner
bending with her kerchief above your patchwork panel
to wipe away dust blown by the wind. Forget

the wind, which was a heckler for speechmakers
at the podium on the south end of the quilt,
causing static to pour from loudspeakers,
blurring tributes with deep thunder rumblings,
making me cough when it whirled toward media
cameramen platformed high over the Great Lawn. Forget

the dust, which was a grasshopper caught in the throats
of singers who tried to inspire the crowd but ended up croaking
like frogs in the pond below Belvedere Castle—
clouds settling on cattails, spreading huge clay-colored wings
over gay couples sentenced to loving
one another in death-row houses.

Among funnel-shaped flurries tugging
at tent pegs which held down the fabric,
threatening to pry it up like a many-colored
flag of The Epidemic to spangle the sky above the park,
I loitered, Milagros Martinez, Donald R. Turner,
telling myself to forget you.

Guatemalan Worry Dolls

The handcrafted dolls
my friend gave guests at her wedding
are tiny enough to keep beneath a pillow.
While I lie asleep,

they worry
and let me dream of banana tree leaves
fanning the rain-forest floor before dawn,
when a rooster

and the strumming
of Hector's guitar in the yard wake Alisa
so gently she steps outside in a crimson
rebozo to say

Buenos días
like a lullaby that is not cut short
by the drumming of soldiers' boots
on the bridge.

The chatter
of gunfire in the village does not echo
through the brush to her thatched hut.
No. She lights

a woodstove
I smell in my sleep—and I dream
my friend's six-month marriage did not
go up in smoke.

Mexico

1

In Mazatlán on their second honeymoon
she lets him speak Spanish to porters
and maitre d's. After he passes
out pesos, she lets him decide
whether to take a taxi to town
or, from their ocean-view terrace, track
the ships that cross the horizon.
That night after piña coladas
when her nerve ends flutter at his touch,
she looks up over his shoulder
at a bright green lizard on the wall.

2

He shuts his eyes and sees a mirror
image of himself, alternating
with a man in a Panama hat, making love
to a platinum blonde. The man's hat
bobs wildly as he takes her from behind,
but the woman pulls away, her wig askew,
as the man loosens his tie.
Only now, atop his wife when he passes
his hand through his own thinning
hair and hears the breakers hit
the beach below their window,
can he come before wilting inside her.

3

Long before her parents' divorce
she used to think serial marriages
had something to do with cornflakes.
Since daughters from broken homes
try to patch up their lives,
she will be patient and strong,
content in this Catholic country
where women lie down for a lifetime.
She will cleave to her husband
like the red bougainvillea climbing
the wall of the Holiday Inn.

4

He knows he loves her well enough
to tell her all his secrets.
The night before their departure
the terrace door is open to ocean
breezes that cool them on their bed.
She sips beer from the mini-bar,
while he empties a pint of tequila añejo
and tells her everything.
She listens. She cries,
and when he finishes speaking she knows
she loves him well enough
to tell him only lies.

5

The day they leave for the airport
the beach is a shining, baked arena.
Beyond the speedboat and water skier
a burnt-sienna island seems to stand
for something they linger for,
some sort of apartness they need
to keep them together.
They love its arid off-limits.
They gaze at its hillside
and tell each other they will return
one day to gaze at it again.

Supper in Tiberias

On the western shore of the Sea of Galilee
a waiter lures you with a loud *Shalom*.
You take a table by the water's edge
and ask about the famed Saint Peter's fish.
They're fresh, the waiter says; they just arrived
this afternoon, an extra-special catch
because the heavy rains this winter helped
them fatten up.
        He grins, and you believe
him when he says a drought exposed pre-Roman
pilings by the shore; a yellow scum
and lower water levels starved the fish
of oxygen for years, but now once more
they're honey-luscious—and for just twelve shekels.
He brings one on a platter with french fries
and sprigs of parsley, head and all, for you
to bathe with juice from lemon wedges.
            You
decapitate and bone it squeamishly,
then savor half-a-dozen mouthfuls, less
than you expected, though the fries make up
for lack of protein with a starchy bulk
you've grown accustomed to in the Mideast.
You pinch your waistline, sip your Goldstar beer,
and think of prehistoric lake beds, half-
aware a cat is staring at your plate.
Beneath adjacent tables three lank tabbies
have crept from nowhere, nonchalantly bent
on filching your leftovers; one by one
they saunter ever closer and meow.
When you say "Scat," they twitch their tails
or yawn outrageously and bare their teeth.

The waiter's gone inside; in a pique
you fling your supper's scraps into the water.
You hear the splash and wait for scavengers,
perhaps Saint Peter's fish themselves, to finish
off their luckless cousin—while the cats
slink off in evening shadows.
                                        You observe
the eastern sky is growing brighter now
and ask the waiter, back with coffee, why.
Are city lights responsible? The hill
beyond the far shore, eerie silhouettes,
resemble scenery in passion plays.
                                        The waiter
winks and says the light's from Syria,
pronouncing it to rhyme with Manchuria,
and you're surprised that such a distant place
—Damascus more than fifty miles away—
produces so much light it swallows stars.
But now you see it's not a city, not
a million Arab lightbulbs, but the full
moon rising over hilltops, laying down
a gold path on the Sea of Galilee.
The moon is walking on the water now
with catfish and Saint Peter.
                                        As you leave,
you ask the waiter what his name is.
                                        He
stares straight into your eyes and tells you, "Simon."

Ammunition Hill

This hilltop park with paths between the trees
was once a Jordanian stronghold. Twenty years
have dried up Six-Day bloodstains and transformed
the minefields into leafy knolls and groves.

My nephew waves for me to run through well-kept
trenches once commanded by the Arabs
before Israeli forces stormed the hill
and bayoneted every last defender.

Now Naim pokes a stick at me and whoops
in Hebrew. Only ten years old,
he does not know the wars his father fought
will be rehearsed in boot camp all too soon,

when, out of high school, in a uniform,
he trades his stick for an Uzi.
Can brothers set aside the holy wars
they waged as children? Forty years ago

no bedroom could contain their rivalry.
They were like Cain and Abel in the fields
their parents planted out of ignorance.
Today my brother lags behind his son,

Naim, who yells and charges toward the massive
Arab bunker, now a war museum.
My brother wanders past a captured tank
on blocks, picks up a stone, and turns to me.

My Mother's Feet

Unsightly, with bunions,
they lost their shape, she says, because of poor-fitting
hand-me-down shoes she wore as a child. How many games
of Kick the Can added to their width I can only guess,
not to speak of the runaway genes of her mother, no sylph.
If the tiny, bound feet of Tang Dynasty ladies seemed lovely,
hers fattened on the sidewalks of Bradhurst Avenue,
one toe poking out of a hole in her sister's sneaker.
Walking to school, she taught rowdy boys to crumple
when their fists missed her and their balls caught her boot.

Now that she's come down with a new bout of cancer,
she says she's just out of breath. She gave up cigarettes,
booze and Unitarianism, as well as the ham-handed
surgeons who sewed her up twice. She'll rid herself of this
old sidekick cancer, this tumor the shape of a soccer ball . . .

Her voice trails off on delicate, hesitant feet.

The Blue Bird Inn

Grandpa, you had it all, right down to the shiksa
bookkeeper, the banker who covered your mortgage.
Your partner looked like a rabbi; your wife
and four kids lived in a clapboard house.
Vegetarians, go home! The Blue Bird Special

was brisket of beef alongside a mound of horseradish.
Honest Yankel from Galicia, you spoke Yiddish
on Sabbath and Yinglish during the week.
Your favorite expression—so my mother tells me—
was "I'm so happy, *meine Kinder*, I kiss you all."

Grandpa, I kiss you for marrying your cousin,
fathering my mother, for feeding them whitefish and challah
on the Bronx's elegant Grand Concourse. I kiss you
for looking the other way while somebody stole your Blue Bird's
golden egg: bushel baskets topped with apples but otherwise
    empty,

chickens not delivered, your partner and bookkeeper
gone, cops shrugging shoulders, sighing, neighbors' kids
crying, "Old Man Blocksberg, on the rocksberg!"
the Blue Bird Inn's doors closing just in time
for the Great Depression to sweep you under its rug.

Game

Before long fall rains will arrive.
Auto mechanics will lower their lifts
and sniff the air, snapping their fingers.

Hunting will be on their minds: Day-Glo
orange vests over their ponchos, shotguns
slung over their shoulders, bird dogs at heel,

they will clasp hand warmers and flasks,
then crouch in duck blinds, assaulting
each other with stories about cars.

Before long they will grow tired; they will smoke
weed by tiny fires and yawn when they see
faces in the flames. Their girlfriends have

left them, their bosses remain to harangue them.
But they've spent enough winters to know
that survival depends on the perfect decoy

and a freezer full of duck.

Woodland Sketches

1

Leonardo's tiny sketches of ravines and river
valleys abound with minutiae: Buds,
stamen and pistil reel
in a wordless dance with his pencil.
Sometimes he used mirror writing to describe
the thermodynamics of curlicued ocean waves.
But mainly he enabled copses
and swales to speak, in chalk
or graphite smudges, for themselves.

2

I have returned to New Hampshire to study
the line and color of mountain meadows
because I no longer look for veins in leaves or thumb
the bristly backs of caterpillars out of curiosity.
I have lost touch with the bark of fir trees.
Yet their needles nettle me with the memory
of nights I camped over timberline
and built fires with pine cones squirreled
away in my knapsack.

3

Last night under a Florentine moon
outside my lean-to on Mount Washington
I pulled quills from my terrier's snout.
Deerflies batted; lightning bugs blinked hard.
Upwind a barn owl signalled
to its ancestor hooting by the Arno.
I waited for daybreak
to redden over granite ledges
as if over centuries.

4

In the bramble behind my campsite
today I fill a baseball cap with berries
that stain its sweatband with their juice.
I return to my rock perch and writing board
by a stand of evergreens
and ravage the capful.
I collect quartz and mica stubble
from the stone's face with my knife,
then nap on a mattress of pine boughs

5

and dream I am a bearded Medici
conferring with an artist about paintings
of popes and courtesans. "The Church,"
I tell him, "shall be favorably portrayed
if possible, but you shall pay attention
to the landscape's odd assortment
of rock formations and twisted rivulets
as subject of a study on its own
or backdrop for a lady's smile."

6

I waken. My dog is asleep, tied to a stump
where day lilies sprout through a knothole. I jog
to the creek: Barkless strips, like driftwood
littering the chinks between boulders,
are evidence of beavers. Prints in sand
belong to a bear whose claws
must have raked the emerald reaches of this pool
for rainbow trout that shot toward darker water,
only to be scooped up flashing in the sun.

Dorland

You can't think of that pine tree by the window
without your mind skipping and scraping over rocks
away from it. Why does the whoosh
of wind in its limbs sound like a waterfall?

And why can't you hear the crazy yip-yap of coyotes
at sundown without thinking it must be a pack of boys
in the ravine pretending to be wolves? You might
as well be wearing earplugs or a blindfold

as dwelling on a mountainside with hawks
and ravens that squawk uniquely,
while, outside your cabin in the darkness, stars
shine like nothing you have ever seen.

～

Like nothing you have ever heard,
the caterwauling of a mountain lion
keeps you awake the night after
your hike to the Far Spring,

where, under a full moon, you caught the glint
of water when a tawny flash in the brush
leaped on another tawny back
and brought it down without a sound.

～

The truth is, you lost your head
when you were a boy pretending to be
Shelley. He could not feel the wind
without thinking of freedom. He could not hear

a bird without naming it "spirit." The truth is,
you lied like him so well you could no longer
distinguish the world from the word,
a bird on the wing from a feathery notion.

∽

This morning the colony cat in the pine
is a vague gray ball. As she clambers
up the trunk, her claws sound like bare
facts sticking to the varnished truth.

When she settles into a crook on a limb
and swishes her tail, her ears lie flat
against the side of her head.
In broad sunlight she stares

you down, yellow eyes unblinking,
without a meow, her mouth curled
into what looks like a grin,
while she asks the riddle you can't answer.

Crabbing

Something about a lighthouse beacon's beam
crisscrossing a path through saw grass
Something about wet sand
on the soles of bare feet
                    padding
away from a white colonial house with a porch
a captain's chair a helmsman's wheel and compass
the telescope on a widow's walk pointing
past land's end past a sea wall
How many sailboats and whalers between here
and the first tiny ice floe
How many islands reefs
wavecrests moon-silver at midnight

      Sunrise: he sculls through mud
      Low tide: he rows then motors
      through brown shallows
                    past a shoal
      where dozens of long-necked geese
      lift off in sync

      A cloud shifts
      His mood thickens
                  It is late
      Already astir in drab carapaces
      from underwater sandcastles males
      are following females
                  sandpipers
      of the saltpond's bottom
                  scurrying
                      from a net

Something about bright netting
to tempt a crab a Cancer like me
Something about star charts and fog
an hourglass emptying
                    onto a continental shelf
How many slips and faults between here
and the last port of call
How many doldrums typhoons
nights alone under Polaris and the Crab Nebula

Eclipse the Dark:
My Fiftieth Birthday, July 11, 1991
(For my mother)

1

The highway pocked with potholes crossed
a sun-beaten plateau, past goats
herded by boys with slingshots,
and men with machetes strapped to their backs
riding burros on the berm.

If that was the royal road from Zacatecas,
I was king for the day, Señor Reyes
in Ray Bans, singing *"Las Mañanitas"*
to myself as I jounced
through towns in my rented car.

I had skimmed through four generations
by noon, recalling my maternal great-grandpa
Obadiah had outridden stop signs
and lived to be a hundred and two.
Now the one-o'clock sky loured;

clouds deepened, amber to umber; shadows
showered mesquite, Joshua trees,
till a false twilight stalled
over a dog baring fangs, stretched
dead in the opposite lane,

and I caught myself in the rearview mirror,
squinting at the penumbral
haze beyond my headlights:
green in the dashboard's glow,
I was halfway home.

2

That black plateau under a skyful of stars,
when I parked, looked like the floor
of a crater greater than I'd ever seen—
as if I could crawl up its walls
to the Milky Way's rim

and study every wrinkle
and river in the Earth's dark caldera.
From a Pemex truck stop I craned
for a glimpse of the total eclipse's
frost-white corona, with prominences,

quarter-million-mile-high
mega-headed fire storms
against a midnight backdrop. The middle age
of a less-than-average superstar
had a dowdy glamor.

In umbral shade I knew
The Woman in the Moon, with a chiseled
profile, whom the Orientals
noticed aeons ago,
was no vestal señorita.

I knew that she and the sun in missionary position
rode the zodiac's pale divan
in fullness once a month, conceiving tides,
the moods of politicians, lunatics
in love with power and light.

3

Moon-shadowed, I wanted to do a hat
dance with Cassiopeia
in stately lazy eights
across a sequined floor
a thousand light years wide,

to wave a red cape at Taurus
and shout *Olé*, jigging
to a quasar's blips, as if one moment of truth
could drive a sword
through a dilemma's horns.

Below galactic nebulae
I wanted to feel neutrinos comb
through my thinning hair
and believe that I was a bald eagle
devouring a snake,

that I was the coffin clasping the corpse
and the womb embracing the fetus,
that my face, round as the Aztec calendar,
was—Montezuma—ageless.
For seven earthly minutes

in darkness I wanted to believe
that I flew at more than light speed
so fast I viewed the past:
the bang, the blaze, the breast
of the new sun suckling planets.

4

Mother, I used to believe you would turn
Quetzalcoatl's tail feather
into a pen to write the Great American Novel.
You played "*Cielito Lindo*" on the guitar
and said the sky was so pretty

over Acapulco that your novel would end
with the words of a widow
at dusk: "*Mira el sol.*"
I borrowed that line in a poem. My dreams
were more vivid back then than my waking days.

But fifty revolutions around a star
eclipsed the dark and made me see
that I could take up your pen
and harness the horse-headed
sun to a thought that set out

aeons ago to brighten on this page,
to flare like a meteor here:
that the light which surrounds us
and comes from within us—false
dawn flooding ditches,

drenching herders, goats—
is a fountain of youth
wherein we shine,
primeval Mother Earth,
shine all the way home.

from Ten Thousand Good Mornings (2001)

My Daughters in New York

What streets, what taxis transport them
over bridges & speed bumps—my daughters swift

in pursuit of union? What suitors amuse them, what mazes
of avenues tilt & confuse them as pleasure, that pinball,

goes bouncing off light posts & lands in a pothole,
only to pop up & roll in the gutter? What footloose new

freedoms allow them to plow through all stop signs,
careening at corners, hell-bent for the road to blaze straight?

It's 10 P.M. in the boonies. My children, I'm thinking
you're thinking your children are waiting

for you to conceive them while you're in a snarl
with my sons-in-law-to-be who want also to be

amazing explorers beguiled by these reckless night rides
that may God willing give way to ten thousand good mornings!

Cycle

What why when where who
I crush my wedding glass beneath my shoe

In with from to at
I kiss my bride & cry Jehoshaphat

Five three four two one
I father daughters & entomb a son

Minsk Flint Perth Seoul Rome
I travel far to find myself at home

Large squat thin fat small
I greet a stranger in a shopping mall

Taste touch smell hear see
I lose my wife my gentle Melanie

I take my life & shake it by the hair
Who what why when where

Woodruff Court

Phooey on rue! The wind's brisk, the sky's blue.
The cul-de-sac smacks of Briggs & Stratton

rotary mowers & Smokey Joes on back patios.
I shall rejoice in the noises & smells

of my neighbors recreating while the ice
cream truck plays "Three Blind Mice"

so eerily that my pet cat behind the couch
sets up a yowl for an unsighted mouse.

Baloney on spumoni! This all-American Good
Humor's no exotic gelato. My little dog laughs

to see such Sunday sports on down-home TV
as I have guffawed at & shall rejoice in

till the sky breaks faith & it rains cats & dogs
& my new-seeded lawn runs away with the water.

Lily

Went out & scissored a lily, brought her inside
to study her fuzzy brown anthers loaded

with pollen, her needle-thin pistil & filaments
down to her ovary. Noted her sepals

were dotted with droplets; her waxy gold petals
were stippled with pigment, the comeliest rust spots,

like freckles on the face of a tomboy agog
in a tree house at twilight. Saw how, twice-dappled

with drizzle & beauty marks, she tilted a bit in her vase
toward my pencil as if she could lift it to write

& tell me the checkered tall story of all things in bloom.
Saw two of her petals were nibbled—by a rabbit? a fawn?

Wrote how she told me she loathed the incessant devouring
mouths which would strip her & call her a woman.

Girls in Rogers Park

stuck twigs up one another's assholes
& clung to each other under a front porch

while their mothers shopped for peanut
butter & gingersnaps.

While their fathers' cars were parked
all day in the Loop for a dollar

girls after school thought
of Dale Evans restless in Evanston

& Roy Rogers riding through Rogers Park
on his horse to play hooky

& spin-the-bottle in secret
with Ginger Rogers who would never spank

him on his penis or yell at them to stop
kissing & clinging under the porch

where they could hide & smile & think of boys
as Buck Rogers & George Rogers Clark.

Volunteers in East Africa Spend the Night
in a Greek-Owned Hotel, Fall 1963

All day driving inland from Dar, peering out their car windows
& that night at the White Horse Inn as the newlyweds tasted

some sweet baklava, there was nothing to worry them more
than how to greet people with *Jambo*, to say in Swahili,

"How far to Songea?" So when they awoke & went down
to a breakfast of grapefruit awash in white sugar, the seeds

were a nuisance but nothing to faze them or make them regret
having left Colorado & college dorms for this hotel-

keeper who said *Kalimera*, then bade them get up
from their coffee to follow him into a back room where they

could digest a report from the BBC on an old wireless
which worried his whole office wall. The report rumbled on

till they couldn't make sense of the English, which sounded like
        Greek:
Dallas sounded like Pallas Athena, the grim motorcade

might have been on an odyssey. Back in their battered sedan
on a narrow dirt track for uncounted kilometers, scrub

& mud huts were a wonder: the woman whose shawl was a rag,
kids naked by water holes, riverbeds—dusty terrain

the must-see moving backdrop for distantly wedded events.
This was their first gritty glimpse of the black underworld.

Lake Street

Sheathed between steak houses
   in his shop under the Green Line,
the sharpener's knife gave off sparks.

   His grindstone spun all day,
large as a roundtable, honing
   ham slicers, meat cleavers.

If it was powered by what made the trains
   screech overhead, their whistles
simulating a scalpel's edge,

   it also seemed to spin because of forces
he knew how to fuse by himself; his fingers'
   grip on steel had just the right pressure.

He was no musician, but every blade
   whetted on his wheel
sounded like more than metal.

   It sounded like something forged
out of tuning forks & good fortune.
   While his knives sparkled,

the sharpener gave in to a dream
   of butcher blocks in chophouses
knocking out the serrated lines

   of an anthem called "Lake Street"
steeped in the water-sweet feel of long green.

Table Talk

In Spanish "Here is a table" sounds like
the Yiddish for "A cow eats without a knife,"

which means that a maitre d'
could usher my mother to lunch

in a café not far from the Prado
& say something she might interpret

as a suggestion to skip the pork sausage
& order the hamburger steak.

No, she never stopped loving the meatloaf
her grandmother baked in Galicia.

I don't mean Galicia, Spain
but the province in southern Poland

where the locals tabled the menu
& decided to knife the kikes.

A Rented House in the Country

Nail a bushel basket without a bottom
to the inside wall of a barn converted
into a garage & do lay-ups when the parked
Ford leaves its stall. Say you are big
for your age, but gawky, a bean pole whose hook
shots swish through a makeshift hoop. Say
you pivot & dribble on splintering planks

while upstairs in the locked loft, under
a floorboard, a canvas bagful of tax forms & cancelled
checks tells how the landlord ducked & dodged
to save his Cadillac from the IRS
before he scored years in the slammer—his candy factory
out back, a green tarpaper shack that sprawled
over an acre, was his front for a smuggling operation
stung by T-men in the Truman administration.

Now that your father has converted one of its ramshackle
storage rooms into an artist's studio,
say his unfinished still life of bananas
& a coconut big as a basketball is sweet
as Batista's regime. Say all the cane sugar
in rum & moonshine, all the impastoed icing
on life's cake, are something you can taste

while you study your father's footwork as he pivots
to gain perspective, then leaps at the canvas
with his palette knife when he adds a palmetto
bush & a man in a Panama hat to the new scene
on his easel—for hours he has been painting
an adobe farm house with a trap door,
a barnyard with chickens & a burro that belongs
to the boy who lives there. Say that boy is you.

Windbreak

Without dope the trees
                across the ravine
   looked like everyday
            hardwoods & conifers.
    Not like an intense
         crowd
             of bystanders belted
into forest-green trenchcoats
            climbing a gusty
      hill. Not
        like characters
in an arboreal
      fable about how limbs give way
              to risk
       because rigidity spells
             axed
        matchsticks.
There was no fire
      only a cold-blooded
           flutter
     a rush
         of slowdowns.
Without dope the trees on the ridge
         looked bosky.
   The porch provided
      an eyeful
        of maples & pines
     spruces & oaks
  he could see
    for themselves
      leaf by needle.

Hotel Giacomo

1

By an arched window the American
                              with a Walkman
         tuned to *Madame Butterfly*
                        has been studying
a building across the street.
                              During Act One
         he lets his eyes caress
                        the limestone
façade which seems to echo
                        Puccini's
         slow crescendo of passion
                        the music a mirror
of Veronese wrought iron
                        fixtures
                              little balconies
         set into a modest palazzo
                        that could be a home
         for unwed mothers.
He takes in all
                three floors & hears
                              Pinkerton singing
                as a fourth layer
         of feelings
                the metamorphosis
in which characters
                are cast
                        into stone which emotes.
         From Mount Fuji's
                        symmetrical
         snow cone (a dormant
                        volcanic
                              blow hole)

                to Vesuvius which buried
                                Pompeii
                in the twinkling of Pliny's
        round eyes
                whether you wear a kimono
    or Navy whites
                love's mega-heat
                            can make you sing
                    your lungs out.
        He knows this
                    as a breather
                            who has collected
                his share of butterflies
                                over the decades'
                    slow crescendo
        to a new theme
                    in a remote key.
                                Right now at a table
                    near the Piazza Bra
                                on a side street
                    overshadowed
        by masonry
                    less Palladian
                                than intimate
                    in its vivid
        honey-yellows
                            a woman
    is unpacking her compact
                        to powder the wings
                of her cheeks.
                            He thinks of her chalk-
                white as a geisha
        sipping tea
                beneath red-tiled
                            roofs

thinks a largo

        their love duet

                soars toward the Alps

         glides higher

     north

        then eastward

            on a whirlwind

& makes a habitation in mid-air.

2

Is this the lie he needs

         to believe he's love's lieutenant

the *dolce far niente*

      with a voice

           to shore

    up that keystone

arch ambition

     which made the great Giacomo

compose?

   È vero

     was his blueprint

for the eternal city

    within him.

Today his namesake

    James

      awoke uneasy.

   Call him the last

     wayfarer

    to think fun

      in a mid-priced hotel room

  is the mezzo forte

     strain

       of a coloratura soprano

                    against the backdrop
     of a house
               whose architecture
                         harmonizes
                                   with her aria.
If this Jimmy-Come-Lately
                         believes the truth lies
                    between
the chips & cracks
                    of stones & tones that split
off on their own
                    is the woman
                              sipping tea near the Piazza Bra
                    invented
                         or real as the rain
     beginning
               to pelt his hotel window
                                   in nervous
                                        bursts?
               This Giacomo unplugs his Walkman
     throws
          open the window & thinks
                              right now a woman must
               be opening
                    her chalk-white umbrella crowned
     with a circle
                    of Day-Glo so red
                              that he can hear it
                              soar
               the color
                    listened-for
                              the rising sun.

Conference Call

1

The feistily fusty book critics & dons,
all tenured, who met in a swank Radisson's

green conference room to discuss the demise
of the avant-garde, managed to mumble & wheeze

through a couple of papers on Gaddis & Gass
before breaking for lunch & exclaiming gee-whiz

they were sick of traditional saccharine words
like "lovelorn" & "sunset" & "motherless kids."

When the open bar beckoned the tongue-weary group
with some mid-day excuse to unbutton the lip

of the bashfulest anti-Romantic, a guy
made a pass at a feminist, saying, "Uh, hey,

have you read any poem as postmodern as *Howl?*"—
to which she replied, "Fuck off, asshole!"

2

Well, dozens of scholars in cultural studies
converged at a punchbowl to trounce fuddy-duddies

& beat up on white males refusing to see
post-colonial lit was the field ripe to be

harvested by Harvard grads, not to speak
of Princetonians, Yale men & women alike.

Not the gurus of Wall Street but Walcott, Kincaid,
& Rushdie would break through tight ethnic blockades.

Don't forget that the stereotyping of Freud-
ians, Marxists, & gay people had long annoyed

the disciples of Benjamin, Weil, & Bakhtin—
deconstructionists, structuralists all in the green

room at the Radisson mixing it up
with martinis, like Martians content to be hip.

3

They were cooler than cubes in the glasses they quaffed
as they mentioned job offers & gossipped & laughed

at old-fogey New Critics & Aristotelians,
their dumb mainstream cousins who clung to the millions

of misunderstandings which governed the Sixties,
whereas now was the time for all scholars to fix P's

& Q's, so the alphabet soup in a dish
could spell out the names of dear Stanley Fish,

Frank Lentricchia, & Marjorie Perloff, as well
as their numberless untenured colleagues in hell

at the podium teaching Comp Rhet to a class
of banana heads registered on a fail/pass.

Don't forget unemployment, the unlisted Schlindlers,
poor colleagues who dreamed they were posh Helen Vendlers.

4

Well, Internet nerds & suave theorists were
just about to convene in the conference room for

Chapter Two of the fête—"Multicultural Proust"—
when the learned assembly was stopped by a blast

from the loudspeakers placed by the dais—& these words:
This is a conference call to the herd

of you smart avant-gardists, a call of the wild
from someone who's hungry for knowledge to feed

his insatiable craving. Virginia & Thomas,
no wolf at the door is as green-eyed, I promise,

as I for your God-given gifts of clairvoyance.
Return now to panels with wit & ebullience.

Break through the sheepfold of muttonheadisms.
My saber-toothed ears are pricked open for business.

Skimming Toward Blue
(Elegy for a Poet)

1

So what if he drank, fucked like a skunk
& stomped on his colleagues also drunk.

He was no vegetarian saint, by God.
No avuncular hubby, he did what he did

because he was smitten by poetry &
a passion for paradise which he designed

by writing & wilding—to hell with the tea
cups & rose hips in drawingrooms. He

was at home on a river bank playing guitar
or in bed with the chairman's wife while her

ponytail played with a line in his head.
No child-murdering creep, he did what he did

because he was still the invincible kid
barnstorming & hellraising until he was dead.

2

If in life he sometimes made good on his word,
kept promises & was faithful in fact

words were what he was best at, finally:
his descriptions of fog not evasions

but a clear lens, a declaration of dependence
on meadows, wet pebbles, & sheep

in the rain rightly rendered, plainspoken
in patters & plinks. Oh he was good

at making myths out of molehills, tunneling
under the truth to uncover a Truth

that belied his deception, his greed for humongous
distortions, & lit up a landscape completely

appointed with moss-mazy rivers
which rippled with riddles yet wound their way home.

3

On the way home in DC the night he clambered
out of my car & planted himself by the gas pumps

he looked like a line backer for the Redskins.
Who calls him a shark in the end zone?

Evenings in Leesburg he fondled the mike
with delight while he rattled off facts,

I thought of him as Commander in Chief.
Who calls him a pig in a war room

of pleasure? Yeah, he spoke about women
in droves. Yeah, he clicked off my tape recorder

& whispered no wilderness glinting with rivers,
no fifth of Glenlivit at the end of the day

could compare with a girl in a black negligee
or an underage boy in a swimsuit.

4

But listen up, friends, if he called himself a fiend
& a monster, in my book he

is a troubadour who will lure us
to hear him again when the tuneless

fin-de-siècle scribblers leave the room.
Soon his split lines crackling like firewood

his anapests' luminous stresses
will light up a landscape where foxes

will lie down with hounds while we stand
up in the millennium, bent on reclaiming

his riverine music, recalling
torrential undercurrents of feeling

he brought to the surface, his silver canoe
abob on white water, Christ! skimming toward blue.

Prelude

"A sculpted rose, the thing itself, its dream . . ."
I wrote those words in college, at nineteen.

I'd just been reading The Republic when
I glimpsed the statue out my window in

the courtyard where my dormitory's quad
gave back the little bit of sun it had

after a day of rain. The figure of
a woman seated on a bench forgave

the twilight as she paused to turn the page
of her bronze volume—was it Coleridge?—

which she'd been reading since my freshman year
& would continue studying while her

metal tresses, permed & passionless,
revived these fourteen lines—ah Kubla, yes!

from Slap Me Five (2002)

Slap Me Five

I believe in the separation of Church & State
as fervently as our Founding Fathers.
But the five Bible verses that each kid read aloud
before our class recited The Lord's Prayer
in home room every day in Hillsdale, New Jersey
let me learn such ravishing Jacobean
English that today I feel like King James
at my keyboard, writing, "Behold,
it is a high-cirrus morning; the sky is white."

No longer a fifth grader—my hair's getting white—
I'm not about to launch a theocracy
& turn my college classes into Christian
gab fests, much less Jewish megillahs.
But when I jog at dawn I think, "My God,
five miles lie before me like five hundred
lines of poetry I learned before I knew
I would be running with the poets who
give us this day our dose of old New Jersey."

Woodcliff Lake

(For Lynn)

Think of the spillway in spring after three days' rain
made the lake overflow in a rush down the concrete sluice.
Either the water whooshed like a mini-Niagara,
or it sounded like wind in the trees when we necked on a bed
of russet pine needles protected from peeping toms.
One week at the end of April eight inches of rain
made up for a two-year drought which had laid bare the parched
reservoir's floor & had let us walk out to a tiny
island the previous fall. In sneakers we'd trespassed
& tramped over powdery clay, over crazy-shaped cracks,
to a coniferous hideout, a Swiss-Family pine grove where we
lay back & yakked about school while a couple of crows,
unseen on the branches of evergreens, cawed, "water water."
The books I'd devoured, *The Yearling* & *Jean-Christophe*,
were on my mind as much as my mouth was pressed
to yours in slippery kisses. A boy & his deer,
in Florida, amid sinkholes & whooping-crane marshes,
still ran through the forest, as Rawlings had written, "forever."
So too Rolland's composer, caught in storm
& stress even after his death, was "soon to be born."
"Forever" & "soon to be born" were my watchwords that fall
when the sun was relentless. The hours we spent alone
on our tree-shaded island seemed all the more precious next
      spring
when rain filled the lake & cut off our access, so we
were forced to find refuge on dry land off Pascack Road
in an evergreen swath, two acres of spruces & firs
planted to shore up the soil by the reservoir's edge.
We lay on our backs & peered up at the pattern of limbs.
One blue-needled spruce was so beautiful you said it looked
like "a huge azure cave." I called it "an Arabic big top,"
though I couldn't explain what I meant, & we suddenly laughed
so loud that a man who must have been napping (or ogling
one of the tattered girlie mags strewn here & there)
under a neighboring tree, yelled "Shit!" & stomped past

our love nest that smelled of blue spruce & eighth-graders'
   sweat.
When *Gone with the Wind* the film was revived that summer,
we read the book. When Sinatra crooned "Young at Heart," we
sang "Fairy tales can come true, it can happen to you" while we
   hiked
west of town through some woods being leveled by workers
   constructing
two lanes that would soon be a turnpike, the Garden State
   Parkway.
That fall we would both go to high school, & you would move
   south,
in our sophomore year, to the Sunshine State. But listen,
our kisses, still out on a limb, will forever remain
in this forest of words, this Arcadia soon to be born.

Edgar Allan Poe Looks Up from His McGuffey Reader

Never alone but in huge groups
                              those blackbirds
                    flew down
     from four-&-twenty
                    nest sites in the North.
     The speckled
                    fledglings
                              flapped over haystacks
                    & corncribs
into bay windows.
                    The dusky adults
               aimed
                    for limbs where they perched
          atwitter
                    on the lookout for cats
                                        then lit
                         into the wind.
               Never
                    alone like robins
          or ravens
     but in swart
               swarms
                    like storm clouds
          those winged
                    featherheads
                              drew near
     swooping & swerving
                    above where he sat
          at his window-side
                    school desk
                              apart.

Getting High in Tyler, Texas

What if the wish of a wussy performer in tow
with his partner, an acrobat, actually happened to grow
into tumbleweed somersaults, thunderous high-wire events
that brought down the house & produced mega-dollars-&-cents?

¡Ay, no me asustes, mi vida!

What if her wrists caught his fingers a hundred feet up
& they pendulumed under the tent as he muttered, "A-yup"
with his New England twang while she sang, "*¿Cómo no?* Willy-
    Poo"
before she flip-flopped & he grabbed both her feet & they flew?

¡Ay, no me dejes caer, mi amor!

What if they tightroped together, both balancing rods
on their palms above onlookers popcorning, snorting, "Ye gods!"
while the ringmaster roared in his megaphone, "Watch, gals &
    guys,
as Conchita & William cheat death high above your bright eyes!"

¡Ay, te adoro, corazón, mi gringo de miel!

O My People

Piggyback, see all the exes, the has-beens we carry.
Our caravan stretches twenty-four/seven from here
to ultima Thule. Our yoke is not easy; with castaway
fetuses, lovers, dead cousins, our burden's not light.

"Giddyap!" they command, these ghost hitchhikers strapped to
    our backs,
while we slog through the sloughs up the high roads. "Let's
    make
it by nightfall!" they snap, so we break out and gallop till dark,
then lie prone and yawn while they yammer and nag us till
    dawn.

Do we dream? Hah, forget it! These great-uncles, backbiters, fat
hangers-on, weigh us down with their stories of honeymoons,
    night-
mares in Gaza, their money-mouthed spiels about going for
    broke—
while we schlep them around all our lives and show off our bad
    luck.

Yippee for the *Demos*

A gang of loud male voices cuts across
my yard & fills my ears. It's four A.M.,
& once again my neighborhood's a zoo
of drunken college students bellowing.
Fuck Tiffany! & *Gimme a brewski, dude!*
top off their tower of babble & describe
a new high point of imbecility.
Are these the scholars Plato wrote about,
whom Socrates engaged in dialogue,
young men who strode through Academe to lead
the polis out of darkness? Dionysus'
wine was nice, you bet your balls,
but men could think, as well as drink, themselves
away from caves, philosophers in love
with light. Tonight's republic has no room
for one pissed poet at the noisy end
of his dead-end street. Greeks & GDIs,
mama's boys & jocks, computer geeks:
I will not stuff my ears with rubber plugs.
I will not call the cops or yell *Shut up*
from my back patio. No, gentlemen,
I'll lie right here in bed & listen to
your goddamned booziatrics till I've learned
to bless you & our great democracy.

Voices

Not far from a brownstone in Brooklyn
Heights where I hailed his cab,

he told me he wrote "voices"
like Marianne Moore & Walt Whitman.

Lines came to him, stuff
he knew he would never "feged,"

not in traffic jams in "Minhattin"
not at home with his Sofie in Flatbush.

Was Sofie a poet? I asked him.
Nah, she was a "dawg," a Great Dane

who listened while he recited Hart Crane
every night in front of a "mirra"

so he could "obsoive" himself saying,
"And yet dis great wink of etoinity."

Riff on Six

All my decades have told me nothing
you couldn't have said in a minute.
Why be at sixes & sevens?
Why sit out a sixth-day evening
away from the merry-go-round?

Lord knows the Earth spins,
& love's the whirligig we cling to
when we're not thinking, "Stick
to intransitive verbs." The object
of Kierkegaard's leap: God's viruses embedded

in human software—let's face it, friend,
we're infected, so why not interface
with fear & trembling, allaying the shakes?
Like black squiggles for diagrammed sentences
or newsprint fork prongs for basketball playoffs,

we're headed for finish lines out there
since Eve launched her sitcom with Adam.
Yet if we end up on the editor's floor
without a kill fee, who wants to laugh? You,
who discovered the grammar of joy

by spooning alphabet soup near a mountain,
were not even six in a high chair.
Now, as we near sixty, valleyed deep,
for the six dozenth time please remind me
how to lift up my eyes to the hills.

≈

Please tell me again that my help
comes from more than a diet of sweat
& obsession—whatever the cure,
may it untie my hands. Please
teach me to get hold of six-pointed jacks:

how to snatch up each gray metal piece
while the ball's in the air; after onesies
through sixsies, how to honor the rules
of "Ring Around the Moon"
& "Shooting Stars." Dexterity,

that dance of dendrites in time
with all things topsy-turvy, lets us play.
Whether we hunker with kids in a schoolyard
or do lunch with lions, the red rubber ball's
what we want not to fall. "Keep it up,"

we tell ourselves, as well as our children,
"you're not about snuff films, glue sniffing,
& AIDS, so, for Pope Sixtus' sake,
bounce back—or, as we said
in the bye-bye '90s, *Get over it*:

the decade's roaring divorces,
relations abloom in a greenhouse of grief.
Get over the hump between morning & night,
the afternoon slump when each Jill & Jack
carries a pail up a hazardous hill."

∿

A new millennium finds fresh faces: Hope
& her step-brother, Nope. She looks forward,
with ice-blue eyes, to chilled-out good feelings,
while he smirks, "nyah, nyah" in a snit.
They argue in Starbucks, sip latte, & grin.

So, too, decrepit sweet-sixteeners,
we've come together—*don't ask me why*—
on patio chairs once owned by Anne Sexton,
after dinner as evening alights. In a trice
you say everything I've tried to express

all my life, & your voice reminds me
of a bird with nine lives, no, a cat
devouring itself with meows. Catbird,
Catullus' catalyst, your uncanny catchwords
resound in my mouth—*don't ask me how*—

whereupon I find myself thinking of six
geese a-laying half-a-dozen eggs near Route 66.
I, who have looked, like a peeping Tom, at nothing
but words, now look to you for sound bites:
a sixth sense whispering, "Yes,"

a sextet for hunting horns & strings,
a star so near that its supernova
takes only six years to reach us in a silent
light show that lasts many moons,
then takes a starry hike—*don't ask me where.*

~

Ask me tremendous rhetorical questions
that stretch past Antares & never arrive
at their hunch-backed question marks:
Hamlet's soliloquy spoken by Harold in Italy,
"Essere o non essere: quello è il problema,"

or your query to me in Verona, Ohio,
"What man art thou?" Ask me what's
in a number: whether I've got sixpence, jolly
jolly sixpence to last me all my life,
or whether I'll rot in a state-run nursing home.

Ask me if I'm caught in Zeno's paradox,
halving my path toward a never-never land;
in Einstein's dream of a theory that could contain
the whole kit bag of space-time & black holes.
Or will you find me now sans final answer,

sans cigar, neither a sextillionaire
nor a master of dactylic hexameter,
while the summer solstice lengthens languidly,
& we sit on your patio to watch
the sixth-month sky aglow? For an hour

we've been out under Venus, viewed the moon
& daylight loitering here. Please tell me how
you grow more lively, beamish, as the sun
hovers like a red rubber ball in the West;
how sixty years are nothing, given this.

Reuven Ben-Yosef

(My brother: 1937–2001)

WAITING

For most of his life, in between—
in a waiting room, reading *Ha'aretz*,
at the market, food-shopping, reciting
a line by T. Carmi, or thinking

up chess moves—he tried to surmise.
He counted off decades, believing
in time's Jaffa orange, fruition,
which meant that his verse, by & by,

might leaven his countrymen's tongue.
He hung in; he liked the word "during."
He held onto "soon" while his children
fared forward, offspring of the moment

that held them like lambs caught in amber
—Mosaic iotas—between
the things of this world & the words
he begat every day at his desk.

WRITING

Kerplunk: he sits down, & the nib
of his pen is already scratching,
scripting trails of indelible ink,
a bloodline that reaches far back

to the Bible & his *Adonai*,
Elohim of his people still seeking
a haven from War & its careless
first cousin, that Jezebel, Rage.

Now his pen is a heavy heads up,
now an ark overflowing with hope.
As he sits, it's as if he is lifted,
made to hover above his new poem,

his diningroom table, his rug
from the States, & then made to float
out the door for a mid-morning stroll.
Clunk clunk: he advances on foot.

WALKING

Note his gait: how he lists to the left,
then lets his weight teeter to starboard.
When he ambles, his shoulders seesaw
with the sidewalk; he wobbles & bobs.

Yet he never hangs back at a crosswalk.
As tough as a long-distance runner,
he barrels through boot camp, through barracks,
hoofing it into a half-track,

firing an Uzi when scrapnel
blows his buddy away right beside him.
From his homeland not known for sashaying,
he goes full tilt, by God, with each foot

landing squarely before him, toward
that absolute back-alley corner-
of-corners, that V in the street,
where he turns & walks out of this world.

WAKING

When he turned & walked out of this world,
he left behind socks, empty shoes;
brined olives from trees near his house;
shelves for the several selves

he conceived while he sat, pen in hand;
the grief of his widow & children;
his terrace above a great rift,
with a view of the dry hills of Moab.

When he lay below Israel's feet,
his blind eyes recaptured the sun;
his deaf ears devised such a vibrant
chorale that it hunted me down

from his valley of shadows, his grave
not a cage. Then I knew that this
was a dream I would see in my sleep
& replay all my days, yea, awake.

Paintable Lady
(My mother)

Cecilia, a 1950s cosmetics queen,
the five-&-dime rival of tonier Estée Lauder—
Cecilia, a kid from Coney Island, jump-started
a business that sold more than lipstick. A bottle blonde
with one huge rouge-red ruby stuck in her brooch,
at three-hour hotel demos in Chicago
when she used balls of cotton to puff on blusher,
the cheeks of Woolworth's salesgirls boldly glowed.
Chain store managers sat through her spiels about women
needing to dream they were lovely: "Beauty's skin-deep
when men are too beastly to see that their ladies have depth.
So paint on rose nailpolish, show off for your customers, honey;
a woman has dreams that are deeper than any man's pockets."
Till the day that she went into debt & was bought out by Cutex,
Cecilia, a minor-league icon, who traded her street smarts
for high heels & hand bags from Saks, as the prez of an outfit
whose products made profit from Philly to the Phillipines,
was glamorous, "mad for magenta," smack-dab in the pink.

Cecilia Products

"Puff 'n' Plush" blushers in purple boxes;
lipsticks: Hawaiian Hues (Aloha Pink, Oahu Red),
or Ice Cream Colors (Peach Sherbet, Cherry à la Mode);
bottled nailpolish remover the color of urine;
no greasy dipilatories, but hair-removing gloves
that left your legs "tingling & smooth";
beige emery boards that treated your nails
to the "finest sandpaper scouring in town";
"Mascara Magic" packaged in black boxes
with cellophane portholes through which brushes
appeared to be floating; eyeliner that made you
"look like Elizabeth Taylor & feel like Cleopatra";
for a buck ninety-nine Cecilia's Very Own Pumice
Stone for unsightly bunyons & corns, so you
could "stand on feet as sweet as a schoolgirl's,
happy right down to your toes."

The Albatross

As if he never earned it, as if she
never told him she was glad,
as if there were no grounds for ownership,
no settled claim, as if she had not murmured, *Sonny,*
shifting in her chair to fix her hair clip,
please wheel me nearer to the picture window
while we discuss your birthright. As if
no one strolled outside, no nursing-home
attendants on their morning break
halted at a crosswalk to point out
white flowers sprouting from a yucca plant.

As if no squealing ambulance sped past,
its rooftop whirligig the color of
arterial sclerosis, while her throat
clogged angrily. As if
no love existed here,
no clean bill.

Nine-One-One Oh-No

Inside the burning Twin Towers
when the workaday lives of three thousand
folks from all over the globe
came together, cremated and crushed
under tons of sheer tumbling rubble,
did they think for an instant of loved ones,
their kids or their siblings, their parents
or partners remarking, *Good morning*
in rooms miles away from ground zero?
Or were their lives snuffed like wax candles
so fast that they had only time
for a final ferocious oh-no,
a curse or a prayer in a flash?
May the strength of their spirits sustain us
survivors of fire and ash!

As Minutes Go By

I'll spend another minute on my wish
to sweep the floor entirely of distrust,
to dust off amity and its big sib,
agape, sitting on the mantelpiece
since Homer sang of war in Ilion.

I'll take the floor a moment to insist
Achilles' wrath, transported to these shores,
will fuel a hundred warships which will miss
the target they should safeguard, helmeted
and handsome in the crosshairs of their sights:

Young Pericles, who built a Parthenon
in each Athenian's top-secret mind,
sought truce with Sparta and brought fourteen years
of peacetime and the seven lively arts
to outposts on the green Aegean Sea.

I'll wave my little flag, an olive branch,
a minute longer, friends. It's Greek to me
how Daisy Cutters, not our kisses, rule;
how time has taught us nothing but a war cry;
how clocks are ticking, *Helen Helen Helen.*

A Child's Garden of Evil

for
Tom Raworth,
Keith Tuma,
and in memory of Reuven Ben-Yosef

Honey and Hemlock

MARCH MADNESS, 2003

The Battle for Baghdad: It looms
Like a minefield of mind-blowing 'shrooms
Now that Bush has allied us with lies
About how Saddam and bad guys
Will unleash dogs of hell to lay waste
Whatever is godly and chaste.

Will Saddam press the buttons to blow
Up the Golden Gate Bridge and Heathrow?
Nope, Bush and his hanger-on, Blair,
Have foreseen the scenario where
Iraq will destroy Brits and Yanks
With its chemical weapons and tanks.

Thus, the Battle for Baghdad begins
Because of the dictator's sins,
His Hitlerian mustache and plan
To replace Bush and Blair with his clan
Who would rule the U.K. and the States
As Islamic emirs, potentates.

But the Battle for Baghdad will end
When we shit on Saddam and defend
What our forefathers meant when they said:
Kill the enemy, yup, kill him dead.
Kill his kids, learn to threaten, then smite—
So that God will bless everyone white.

ANTHEM

Oh, say can you see
How we don't disagree
When we yammer and yak
About cads in Iraq
While so proudly we stand
For truth, liberty, and
Everything they oppose.
Just observe Saddam's nose
Lengthen when he denies
He is reeling off lies.
Just watch women retreat
Behind long robes and cheat
When they cover their faces
And say that no place is
As wondrous today
As the U. S. of A.

When the rockets' red glare
Blinds Saddam, don't you dare
Disagree it is good
He is gone and we should
Spread democracy to
Every villager who
Was a Muslim but now
Will milk cash from the cow
We have specially priced
In accordance with Christ.
For the land of the free
—You will not disagree—
Must ring out with our sneezes,
God-bless-you's, and Jesus;
Must be pure as George Bush
From his *tête* to his tush.

COLLATERAL DAMAGE

Why fret when a misguided missile
Kills a widow in the dark?
Listen, you can hear the whistle
Of a bomb that's off its mark.

She would have died at any rate,
Just as her daughter and her son
Would certainly have met their fate
In a regime ruled by a gun.

Who knows but that she'd shoot us down
If shoes were on the other feet
And our skin, not white, were brown?
She'd murder us, you bet your sweet-

And-sour chicken. She would make
A Yankee pot roast of us all,
Then feed us to her dogs and take
No pity on Paulette or Paul,

Americans who perished when
Her restless pet Kalashnikov
As if by accident—amen!—
Pulled its own trigger and went off.

WMD

I know we're being more than just polemical
When we accuse them of possessing chemical
Defenses. Though we've found no hide nor hair in
Weapons storage dumps, we know there's Sarin,
Mustard gas, and noxious airborne crud
Which would make Allah blush, then cough up blood.
God help us if we breathe it in one day
Without our masks! Then, too, their rich array
Of anthrax-smallpox goodies makes us feel
That mass destruction is no myth; it's real.

Yet we have bunker busters that weigh tons.
Along with Daisy Cutters, we have guns
Whose massiveness, despite their tag, "conventional,"
Is mega-monstrous, omni-three-dimensional.
Remember our new MOABs, bombs so big
They'll level countless football fields and dig
Calderas deep enough to keep a crew
Of workers busy with bulldozers to
The end of time. God help each poor Iraqui
If we turn Baghdad into Nagasaki!

Making Do with DU

If you're lucky enough to get hit in the cranium,
The bullet that's tipped with depleted uranium
Will make the best dent, though your helmet's titanium.

Technicians who brought us U-238
Knew that lead's density was not really so great.
Depleted uranium set the lab straight.

Now metals combined with what's known as DU,
Nearly dense as a diamond, will leave residue
Causing cancer, contaminents, birth defects, too.

There's no need to worry when we fire guns
With depleted uranium. Foreign-born sons,
The mothers of Satans, Attila the Huns,

Are in need of depletion; we're here to assist them.
If we've managed to shoot and wounded or missed them,
DU is the best way to fully enlist them.

Lip service is what we can hope to avoid
From the corpses exploded by missiles alloyed
With DU which honors the years, undestroyed.

We've left our imperial red-white-and-blue
In foreign soil radiant, seething with goo
For millennia—buried alive with DU.

NEWSPEAK

The brass have said it's time to put aside
The old term, *friendly fire*. Now *fratricide*
Is what they call it when, say, Kurdish troops
Are killed by cluster bombs dropped by our stupes.

Or else it's our own klutzes who shoot guns
That accidentally kill Americans.
No matter how you put it, the old fable
Stays the same: it's Cain who's offing Abel

In a field away from Mom and Dad.
Yet Cain rose up, the Good Book says, and had
His way with Abel by no accident.
Do Yanks kill Brits because of ill intent?

Do Arabs shoot their brothers by mistake?
Do Baath officials goof up when they take
Out dissidents, then turn around and shoot
Each other accidentally in the snoot?

If brotherhood is rife with fratricide,
If friends resort to killing, then Christ lied
When His *Love One Another* seemed to say
That war and deadly gaffs would go away.

I don't know who hoked up the phrase *Shit happens*,
But evidently crap wins out—and crappens!

GIN RUMMY

Don Rumsfeld! You're high-powered, that's for sure!
You wrestle with huge weapons, while you lead
Us through miasmal waters to the pure
Anointment that is peace, so that we need
Not worry something filthy like manure
Will coat our spotless jackboots on the shore
Of beachheads ravaged by unholy war.

You're neither hawk nor dove. You are an owl
Hoo-hooing wisely in the sacred dark.
Resisted by that high priest, Colin Powell,
You teach us prudence, never to embark
On sabor-rattling that could disembowel
Us on the tips of hidden bayonets
Held by muezzins in foul minarets.

Only an epic poem could suffice
To point out you're a genius, not a dummy.
Accompanied by Condoleezza Rice
And General Tommy Franks, ah yes, dear Rummy,
You're everybody's image of the nice
Guy who's no chump, no wimp like Jimmy Carter.
If God is smart, by golly, Don, you're smarter!

I Want to Marry Ari

I never met a fellow nicer
Than the spokesman, Ari Fleischer.
Although I've heard it said he's called
A saber-rattler who is bald,
A PR expert who is glib,
I've never heard him twit or fib.
He tells it like it is and says
What he's been hearing from the prez,
Who, trusty as a voting booth,
Speaks nothing but the gospel truth.

I heard a drunk once yell out, "Ari,
Please commit—hic!—hari-kari.
Please for once just call in sick
And leave off telling whoppers—hic!
Word has it there's a woman who's
Your stand-in. Does she guzzle booze?"
I thought that drunk was déclassé
I kicked him in the ass, and, hey,
I'll boot you, too, if you're not nice or
Cast a slur on Ari Fleischer.

COOKING UP TROUBLE AT THE WHITE HOUSE

One day while standing by the stove,
I stirred a pot and blushed deep mauve.
I said, like Zadie Smith, *By Jove,*
I think I've found a treasure trove
Of evidence that one man drove
America to wreck its cove,
The White House kitchen where it strove
To roast a lamb that had the cloven
hoof of that one man, Karl Rove.

I peered into his pot and saw
A floating plasticine last straw
Atop a leg of lamb so raw
No connoisseur from Witchita
Or hungry mullah from Lahore,
—No starveling who's a carnivore—
Could stomach the tyrannosaur-
us rex Rove's telling all us poor
Buffoons is lobster thermidor.

Rove fried McCain and Gore for Bush.
Rove's not the head chef, yet he'll push
His menu on the Hindu Kush,
Romanians who live in Cluj,
And Michael Jordan saying, *Swoosh!*
Rove's methods aren't at all hush-hush.
He never learned to bow or blush
While stirring up his bloody mush.
He shits but knows just how to flush.

LIBERATION

Now that we have liberation,
We must learn our occupation
Is to occupy the nation
We have conquered. Subjugation
Is the wrong term for salvation,
Just as Islam's desecration
Means Redemption in translation.
English offers consolation
To bad Arabs whose low station
Was assured throughout creation
By our Christian affirmation
That the Koran's dedication
To Muhammad meant damnation.

Now that our relentless raiders,
Bible-toters and Darth Vaders
Playing war games like third-graders,
Have invaded, are invaders,
We must call ourselves crusaders
Or brave-hearted soldier-traders
Who will pay. No Arab-haters,
We are truly saints, Ralph Naders
Celebrating Mass and Seders
With Iraquis: bikers, skaters
Full of Yo's and *See you later*'s,
Loving, loved emancipators
Armed with brains like mashed potaters.

READING THE TEA LEAVES

Forget about the tepid word, *Preventive!*
Our policy is, as you know, preemptive.
This means we shit on them before they shit
On us. It doesn't take a lot of wit
To know who's poised to sully us. Call him
Hassan who lives in Syria or Kim
Who's sipping tea, just happening to see a
Chance to waste us from vile North Korea.
You're right in thinking that our veep Dick Cheney
Deplores the sins of dead guys like Khomeni
So much he wants to cluster-bomb Iran.
He'll take out terrorists in Pakistan,
Then go on, numb with fervor's anesthesia,
To drop MOABs on Muslim Indonesia.
Meanwhile, Old Europe, for its peacenik stance
Will get the ax: first Germany and France,
Then Mother Russia. Lastly, he will fine the
Wretched dissidents in mainland China
By bombing them to smithereens in case
They turn around and fling bombs in our face.
Of all preemptive warlords, Wolfowitz,
So scared he'll lose face, covered with the shits,
Will urge our prez to bunker-bust Great Britain
Before it shits on us for all our shittin'.
If you dare disagree with what we're sayin',
We'll bomb you first and never stop hoorayin'!

No Coffee for Kofi

Come closer, girls and boys, so you can hear a
Story I recorded from a man in
Lebanon who worked for Al Jazeera.

One day while walking home, he said he ran in-
to a famous person, and he tripped.
He saw the famous guy was Kofi Annan

Sprawled on the sidewalk, too—alas, he'd slipped.
So the reporter laughed and said, "Hey, Kofi,
Didn't I bump into you in Egypt

Last year, in Alexandria. Go fi-
gure how two guys like us by chance can meet
Here in Beirut! Let's go for Turkish coffee.

Let's chat about old Babylon, Tikrit,
The bombed-out neighborhoods and railway stations
Where no one's going anywhere. Let's eat

Falafel wrapped in pitas, no K-rations,
No junk food for two classy dudes like you
And me who work for the United Nations

And Al Jazeera. Too bad I can't bike you
To a teahouse in dear old Japan in
Spring to sip some oolong and write haiku,

Entering the literary canon
Alongside Dante, Twain, and Annie Proulx."
To which Kofi replied, "Fuck off, Abdul!"

Touring the Lily Pads

It's great to travel to new places
To meet Yanks and foreign faces
In the military bases
We've just opened where the aces
Flying jets go through their paces
Right beside the hardcore cases:
Turkmen, Kurds, the other races
Who run errands, wild goose chases
For us and pretend that grace is
Bowing, hiding all the traces
Of their brittle carapaces.

For their very own protection
We have built up a collection
Of departments of correction
Till our forces set these dreks on
Courses where a fair election
Choosing leaders for inspection
Saves them from dumb insurrection.
This is why you see an X on
Maps we've drawn with much affection
Where our bases meet objection
From no terrorist or Texan.

There will be no intifada.
Fedayeen will see that nada
Can outshoot our huge armada—
It's no game show, no regatta:
Cobras, Warthogs, and a lotta
Rockets launched that would give God a
Bellyache or else give Sadda-
m pains so bad he'd say, *I gotta*

Hit the potty-poo. It's not a
Question of a bad tomahta
But of hellfire, yadda yadda . . .

THE IMPORTANCE OF MARSHES

The other day I asked to share ribs
With a table of marsh Arabs.
They told me, "Hey, man, go to Hades!"
Then they groused that the Euphrates
Met the Tigris in a harsh
Sahara that was once a marsh.

I offered them a slice of challah,
Which they spat on and said Allah
Tried to block Saddam Hussein
When he decided he would drain
The marshes where men fished and poled
Their boats for centuries untold.

I said, "C'mon, you guys're joking!"
Then Masudi started poking
Me, as did all seven others.
"Stop!" I cried. "You are my brothers:
Ishmael and Isaac grew
Up in one household just like you

And me with Papa Abraham,
Both circumsized, not eating ham,
With different mamas, to be sure,
But let's be pals, Shaheed, Mansur.
Let's never once again be harsh.
Let's fill our desert with a marsh."

IN PRAISE OF SAM HAMILL

Mid-April's come and gone. The lilacs show it,
As do the Judas trees, but what in sam hill's
Going on with someone who's terrific,
Who lives in Washington by the Pacific?
This spring's been rough on him, too, as a poet.
As lovely as it is, it's made Sam Hamill
Get down from Pegasus to ride a camel
Through souks and streets so bombed-out and horrific
His rage is endless, and he lets us know it.

He tells us National Poetry Month's a sham
If we can't teach our verses to make war
On jingoistic boneheads who would change
Regimes to suit their needs and rearrange
The seasons, bidding spring and summer, *Scram!*
It's winter in DC forevermore.
O academic poets on the shore
Of oceans near and far, home on the range,
Sam Hamill's cursing. Hear him: *Sing goddamm!*

ZONKED

I never thought a war would wake me up
From dreams of olive branches by the sea.
I sip black coffee from a bitter cup.

The commandant pontificates, "A-yup,
Now's not the time for dozing. Look at me.
I never thought a war would wake me up."

His minions listen. While they sit to sup
On sweet potatoes and molasses tea,
I sip black coffee from a bitter cup.

His mistress knows at heart he's just a pup
In need of petting. "Woof!" she snarls; then she,
Who never thought a war would wake her up,

Yawns over her pink lady—hic, hiccup!—
And draws him to her bosom drowsily.
I sip black coffee from a bitter cup,

Which runneth over every time I sip.
I'm lost between the letters A and Z.
I never thought a war would wake me up.
I swig black Lethe from a loving cup.

MOVING RIGHT ALONG

The world moves on. Our honchos smoke cigars,
Wait for the buck's rebound, the euro's dip.
We've turned our gaze away from war to SARS,
But no one knows which way the leadership
Will take us. Will it be to Venus? Mars?
Or will our macho chiefs give us the slip,
Retreating from the evening news to cars
And Airforce One wherein they'll take a nip
Of pulque with Viagra while the stars
Erupt like ack-acks—or a radar's blip?

One sure thing we can bet on is turmoil,
A shaky deck of cards, a toppled head
Of state the ace of spades who may embroil
Us in more monkeyshines unless he's dead
Or exiled to an island called Trompe L'oeil,
Which Homer sidestepped in *The Iliad*.
There's no avoiding what enthralls us: oil.
Two bucks a gallon makes us all see red.
We'll stay in Baghdad, never to despoil
Prosperity for Arthur and Ahmed.

Another hundred years, and we'll be sheiks
In flowing checkered headdresses with wives
Who mince and mope while everybody speaks
Amerilish, our home-grown tongue that thrives
In Omaha, as well as schlock boutiques
From Marrakesh to Malé where our lives
Will blend with conquered Arabs, Jains, and Sikhs,
Whoever will get rich from what derives
From oily handshakes and our breath that reeks
Of dead meat in a culture that survives.

The Nightshade Arias

UNITED STATES
(Tune: "America the Beautiful")

Oh, Brits and Yanks, heroic guys
Who cause civilians pain,
Who listen to their dying cries
And say, "Hi!" like John Wayne:
United States, United States,
Shoot quick and watch with glee
How politics
Excludes all pricks
From Maine to East Chinee.

Oh, senators and congressmen
Who vote to fund a war,
Who give the nod again—again!—
To deficits galore:
United States, United States,
Spend more than you take in
So that our kids
Will hit the skids
From Bangor to West Linn.

Oh, President, George W
Who changes a regime
Who says, "Hot damn, I'll trouble you
To root for our home team":
United States, United States,
Take aim with Abrams tanks,
And kill or maim
In Jesus' name
With our sincerest thanks.

OFF WE GO
(Tune: "Off We Go Into the Wild Blue Yonder")

Off we go into the wildest blunder
Since the war in Viet Nam.
Helped by Brits and by the boys Down Under,
Minus gooks, minus napalm,
With AWACs, choppers, and with such wonder
Planes as Stealths known as B-2s,
Our drop-dead shock-and-awe tactics
Are on the nightly news.

If you say that these grim prophylactics
Won't stop seeds of Muslim hate
From becoming a huge, dogmatic
Anti-Yank aggressive state,
This is just a matter of your syntactics:
Put the cart after the horse,
Which drops its payload of freedom
Thanks to our great Air Force.

Rest assured that we know how to feed 'em
Rounds galore from Gatling guns,
Rockets, bombs, and enough lead to bleed 'em
Into pulp because of tons:
Dynamite, spent nuclear fuel will speed 'em
To accept our terms of course.
They'll think we love 'em and need 'em.
They'll worship our great Air Force.

THE OBSCENE HYMN
(Tune: "The Marine Hymn")

From the stalls of Muslim Russians
To the slums of Michoacan,
We will blast our dark-skinned cousins
To defend the Son of Man.
First to fight for pure Caucasians
And remain blond-haired, round-eyed,
We will crush all Amerasians
And minorities worldwide.

Here's to health and six Mercedes
For each family of five
So that all white men and ladies
Can fight off the blahs and drive
To their gun shops to protect them
With M-1s and RPGs,
To shoot back at those who wrecked them:
The bad blacks and worse Chinese.

From the ranks of hooded legions
Of Cross burners, may a torch
Light the way throughout all regions
Looking out from their back porch
At the hordes of colored people
Threatening everyone blue-eyed.
Let us blast them from our steeple
Of belief in homicide.

ANCHORS HOORAY
(Tune: "Anchors Away")

Anchors hooray, oh boy!
Anchors hooray!
Last time we missed Hanoi,
But with George Bush we may-ay-ay-ay
Drop anvils on Sainte Foy
Or Mandalay.
Just hear us cry ahoy:
We're here to ship your corpse home to LA.

Keels, masts, and hulls of tubs,
Shipmates at play,
We're here to sail in subs
Whose missiles seem to say-ay-ay-ay
God damn well pounds and drubs
Those in His way,
Arabs and Beelzebubs,
His enemies in Cairo and Bombay.

Sail on and on, my sons.
What can I say?
You're here with megatons
Of stink bombs A-OK-ay-ay-ay.
Battleships', cruisers' guns,
Carriers, hey!
Sail on like everyone's
Example of a murderous cliché.

AMERICA
(*Tune: "God Save the Queen"*)

My country, 'tis of thee,
Land of hostility,
Of war I sing.
Land where appeasement died,
Land where I prayed that I'd
Once more see greed and pride
Ennobling

My native nation free
To bomb the enemy
And be revered.
I love thy streets and streams,
Thy founding fathers' dreams,
And thy commander's schemes
Are nowise weird.

Let my song bring at least
Doom to the Middle East
So that the beer
May at last freely flow
When ruthless rulers go
And thy troops overthrow
Evil and cheer

My country right, not wrong:
Of thee I sing this song,
God-blest, hear hear!

BATTLE HYMN
(Tune: "The Battle Hymn of the Republic")

Mine ears have heard the story of the coming of the troops.
They have flown on crates and Cessnas, they have sailed on rafts
    and sloops.
They have stood alone with rifles, they have fought like fiends in
    groups.
Their guns shoot on and on.

Gory story hallelujah,
Troops have landed here to rule ya.
Don't let nonagression fool ya:
Their guns shoot on and on.

Mine eyes have read the words that Julia Ward Howe wrote and
    sang.
She was born before the terrorists in Baghdad and Pyongyang.
They have taught us nothing sings like guided missiles that go
    bang.
Our bombs drop on and on.

Hoary story O hosanna,
We fly over and drop manna.
To cause Pax Americana
Our bombs drop on and on.

In the loveliness of pine groves on a mountain Uncle Sam
Came alive with nephews, nieces who vociferated, Damn,
Let us spread our family values to Somalia and Siam.
Our seeds go sprouting on.

Hunky-dory holy cowpie,
Wheresoever rooks and crows fly,
We have sired a race that won't die.
Our seeds sprout on and on.

GOSH YES AMERICA
(Tune: "God Bless America")

Gosh yes America,
I see big birds
Fly beside you
And guide you
With the bombs that they scatter like turds.

From cruise missiles
Winging over,
Making whistles
As they fall,
Gosh yes America,
Your big birds all
Spread freedom everywhere
In one fireball.

Gosh yes America,
Feathered with steel
Built by Boeing,
You're going
To shoot ducks on the ground—it's surreal.

From the urban
Roosts of Satan
To exurban
Cuckoo nests,
Gosh yes America,
My right wing rests
On Armageddon now,
Which God requests.

Carols for Caligula

EPISODE IN MOSUL
(Tune: "Away in a Manger")

Away where a ranger shot bullets of lead,
The little Akil lifted up his sweet head.
The stars in the sky were asleep when a round
Took off with his noggin with scarcely a sound.

The chickens were clucking, the sheep made a squall
When the little Akil's head rolled by like a ball.
I love thee, Akil, cried the ranger, Bill Blake.
I aimed for Saddam but got you by mistake.

Be near me, Akil,
Bill Blake started to say,
Close by me forever
And ever a day—

When an RPG hit him
Smack-dab in the mouth
And blew him all over
East, west, north, and south.

VIOLENT NIGHT
(Tune: "Silent Night")

Violent night, lowly night,
All is bombed, nothing's right.
Round yon urchins, soldiers defiled
Mosques and palaces beautifully tiled.
Weep and nevermore cease,
Weep for the downed mantelpiece.

Shepherds and sheep gather in groups,
Witnessing foreign troops.
Round yon village squares Yankees go home
To their barracks to brush up and comb.
Weep and nevermore cease,
Weep for the shorn-away fleece.

Tylenol night, Valium morn,
All is shocked, all is shorn.
Round yon minarets mullahs decry
Streets where shrapnel and dead bodies lie.
Weep and nevermore cease,
Weep for the unlasting peace.

WRECK THE WALLS
(Tune: "Deck the Halls")

Wreck the walls with one long volley.
Toodle-oodle-ooh-dle-oodle-ooh.
'Tis the time to kill, by golly.
Toodle-oodle-ooh-dle-oodle-ooh.

Aim we down our rifle's barrel.
Toodle-ooh-toodle-ooh-toodle-ooh.
Whether we are Carl or Carol.
Toodle-oodle-ooh-dle-oodle-ooh.

Shoot protesters who annoy us.
Toodle-oodle-ooh-dle-oodle-ooh.
That's why Rummy's bums deploy us.
Toodle-oodle-ooh-dle-oodle-ooh.

Don, we now know why we're wreckers.
Toodle-ooh-toodle-ooh-toodle-ooh.
We are not here to play checkers.
Toodle-oodle-ooh-dle-oodle-ooh.

BOY, IS THE WORLD
(Tune: "Joy To the World")

Boy, is the world retarded, dumb.
It can't stop making flak.
Let everyone prepare to come
From countries in true Christendom
And kill so we can sack
Mean rulers and fight back
Regimes ruled by Saddamites and Jacques Chirac.

Oy, is the earth a stupid boob.
It can't sit down and talk.
Let every stupe believe the rube
Pontificating on the tube
Who says he wants to walk
Or fly from Kitty Hawk
To slaughterhouses stinking of raw pork.

He rules the world with class and race
And conquers to stay free.
Let everyone respect his grace,
His handsome Lone-Star baby face
And let his majesty
Go on at least to be
Our very own emperor based in DC.

THE TWELVE DAYS OF BATTLE
(Tune: "The Twelve Days of Christmas")

On the first day of battle the White House gave to me:
A sore bottom in a Humvee.
On the second day of battle the White House gave to me:
Two Tylenols . . . etc.
On the third day of battle the White House gave to me:
Three gross meals . . . etc.
On the fourth day of battle the White House gave to me:
Four busted trucks . . . etc.
On the fifth day of battle the White House gave to me:
Five fifths of gin . . . etc.
On the sixth day of battle the White House gave to me:
Six bouts of shittin' . . . etc.
On the seventh day of battle the White House gave to me:
Seven Kurds hoorayin' . . . etc.
On the eighth day of battle the White House gave to me:
Eight snipers' snipin' . . . etc.
On the ninth day of battle the White House gave to me:
Nine air strikes missin' . . . etc.
On the tenth day of battle the White House gave to me:
Ten kicks from Rummy . . . etc.
On the eleventh day of battle ole Blair House gave to me:
'Leven howls from Cheney . . . etc.
On the twelfth day of battle my war stint gave to me:
Twelve dozen hemmorhoids . . . etc.

JINGO YELLS
(Tune: "Jingle Bells")

Jingo yells, Jingo yells,
Jingo whoops hooray.
O what fun it is to run
A B-1 A-OK.

Jingo yells, Jingo yells,
Jingo hollers, Hey!
O what fun it is to stun
Rogue nations in his way.

Death for everyone,
Tracers on display,
Promising to gun
Terrorists and say,

Fuck the morning sun,
Night's a holiday
Till his mission's gone and done
And he's back on old Broadway.

Jingo yells what-the-hell's,
Jingo loves to play.
O what fun it is to run
A bomber yippee-yay,

Jingo yells his Noëls,
Jingo's not blazé.
O what fun to shoot a ton
Of ammo and to spray

Rounds from gunship's wings
Streaking through the night,
Strafing kids and things
That don't want to fight.

Soon the ding-a-lings
Vanish out of sight
Till he sees dim flickerings
Of Miss Fatima Bright.

Jingo swells, Jingo yells
Out his big bomb bay,
Opens up to drop his shells
On the gal he'd like to lay.

Jingo yells decibels
To the Milky Way.
O how bad it is he smells
As he farts and streaks away.

Printed in the United Kingdom
by Lightning Source UK Ltd.
9665200001B/301-323